YOUR PROSPERITY
BLUEPRINT

*How to Go From Where You Are
to the Level of Success God Intended for You*

JASON HALE

NEW YORK

YOUR PROSPERITY BLUEPRINT
How to Go From Where You Are to the Level of Success God Intended for You

by JASON HALE
© 2012 Jason Hale. All rights reserved.

Unless otherwise specified, all scripture contained herein is taken from King James Version.

ISBN 978-1-61448-065-5 Paperback
ISBN 978-1-61448-066-2 eBook
Library of Congress Control Number: 2011932072

Published by:
MORGAN JAMES PUBLISHING
The Entrepreneurial Publisher
5 Penn Plaza, 23rd Floor
New York City, New York 10001
(212) 655-5470 Office
(516) 908-4496 Fax
www.MorganJamesPublishing.com

Cover Design by:
Rachel Lopez
rachel@r2cdesign.com

Interior Design by:
Bonnie Bushman
bbushman@bresnan.net

In an effort to support local communities, raise awareness and funds, Morgan James Publishing donates one percent of all book sales for the life of each book to Habitat for Humanity.
Get involved today, visit
www.HelpHabitatForHumanity.org.

This book is dedicated to my Lord and Savior Jesus Christ who saved my life, accepts me for the person that I am, taught me to prosper, lifted me from poverty and caused me to stand before kings.

I love you dearly.

ACKNOWLEDGEMENTS

---⊕---

I'd like to say a heartfelt thank you to the following people...

To my wife, Angela, who tirelessly worked around the clock with the children to give me room to focus. Her sacrifice has made my journey much easier.

To my children, who with great anticipation, for years encouraged me to publish this book. Their persistence would not let my ideas die.

To Adria Mitchell, who helped me to word my message in such a way to appeal to a larger audience.

To Terri Liggins, Copy Editor Extraordinaire, who worked tirelessly to edit my manuscript to make it what it is today.

I stand amazed.

TABLE OF CONTENTS

⊕

PART III – Principle #2 The Principle of Saving

PART IV – Principle #3 The Principle of Agreement

PART V – Do things differently

Introduction

A MATTER OF CHOICE

⊕

Foundation Scripture: Deuteronomy 30:19

"...I have set before you life and death, blessings and curses. Now choose life..." (NIV)

One day, quite a few years ago I experienced a true revelation. Perhaps you know exactly what I'm talking about—a thought enters your mind that isn't a new thought, by any means, but rather an old concept with brand new clarity. That clarity gives such an awakening to your spirit that you know it is right to act on it.

Here's the concept that became clear to me that day: life is a sum total of the choices we make. Hmm. Just let your mind camp on that statement for a moment so it can sink in. What it's saying is that our achievements and failures are largely matters of our own God-given choices. We get no more and no less out of life than what we put in to it.

I used to think that outside circumstances—or fate as we sometimes call it— determined where we would end up in life and what we would go through. But not anymore! I now know that what we *do* or *don't* do determines our outcome.

1

When God created us in His own image and after His likeness, He gave us the ability and freedom to make choices just as He makes choices. What I realized is that life is full of choices and we *choose* the life we live.

Do you remember Adam and Eve in the Garden of Eden? When the Lord created the Garden of Eden, He planted the Tree of Life and the Tree of the Knowledge of Good and Evil in the middle of the garden. Adam and Eve could have eaten from the Tree of Life and lived victoriously forever. However, they made a bad choice. They chose to disobey God's command and eat fruit from the forbidden tree - the Tree of the Knowledge of Good and Evil.

What if Adam made a different choice? Can you imagine a world with no war? No crime? No hunger or poverty? Can you imagine a world where all things live in perfect harmony, peace and love?

Do you see now the *real* power of choice? I say *real* power because the way our lives play out is not based on just our own choices but also on the choices *others* make - others such as Adam and Eve. Let's look at another illustration of this power of choice.

In the book of Deuteronomy, Moses gave final instructions to the children of Israel before Joshua led them into the Promised Land. He reminded them that their aimless, yet miraculous, journey through the wilderness resulted from the choices their parents made. Because of that, none of those who lived in Egypt would be privileged to step foot in that Promised Land. When Moses conveyed God's promise to them of a bright future if they obeyed Him, it became their choice. Therefore, choices as illustrated by Moses' message are not to be taken lightly. The choices we make today determine whether we succeed or fail tomorrow.

The purpose of this book is to share with you "The Formula for Success" God revealed to me on that life-changing day in August 1992. Though I did not fully understand it then, I clearly do so now, which compels me to share it.

As part of this formula, I will also expound on the three principles that God promised to command His Blessing upon. Just like the rain that arbitrarily falls on anyone who will step out in it these principles will saturate success upon anyone who chooses to practice them. They are designed to make you wealthy in every area of your life- but *only* if you choose to follow them to the letter.

Most importantly, while you read these pages, bare in mind prosperity is not limited to finances. What good is it to have financial prosperity if we cannot enjoy it because we are failing in our health or in our relationships with family and others? Remember this: money—and the benefits it brings—makes you comfortable, not happy. Happiness can only originate from within.

The Bible says it is God's will for us to prosper and be in health even as—or to the same degree—that our soul (mind) prospers. "The Formula for Success" is a God-given formula. If you choose to follow this formula, you will prosper in your thinking; which will cause every area of your life to prosper in direct proportion. Now that would be a wise choice to make!

PART ONE

FORMULA
FOR SUCCESS

THE FORMULA FOR SUCCESS

---------------------------------- ⊕ ----------------------------------

Foundation Scripture Joshua 1:7-8

"Only be thou strong and very courageous, that thou mayest observe to do according to all the law, which Moses my servant commanded thee: turn not from it to the right hand or to the left, that thou mayest prosper whithersoever thou goest. This book of the law shall not depart out of thy mouth; but thou shalt meditate therein day and night, that thou mayest observe to do according to all that is written therein: for then thou shalt make thy way prosperous, and then thou shalt have good success."

The Lord gave Joshua "The Formula for Success" when He instructed him, *"Only be thou strong and very courageous, that thou mayest observe to do according to all the law, which Moses my servant commanded thee: turn not from it to the right hand or to the left, that thou mayest prosper whithersoever thou goest."*

First, God told Joshua **what** to do: *"observe to do according to all the Law which Moses My servant commanded thee."*

It doesn't get any more plain and simpler than that. No one could work that formula for Joshua; no one can work it for us. If we want a successful life, we have to go after it. No one can win the game of life for us any more than they can cause us to lose it.

Secondly, God told Joshua exactly **how** to do it: *"This book of the Law shall not depart out of thy mouth, but thou shalt meditate therein day and night…"*

In other words, the biblical principles should not stop coming forth out of Joshua's mouth, nor out of our mouths. He wanted Joshua to confess the scriptures and to speak them continually. Then God tells him to meditate in it day and night.

The word, "meditate" in this context means we must speak God's Word to our selves within our selves, to give God's Word deep and considered thought. We must ponder and reflect on it all the time, so that we may observe to do according to all that is written therein. Do you think that is possible to do? It's not *im*possible, but it is a matter of how badly we want what God has promised us.

Lastly, God even graciously told Joshua **why** he should do these things: *"… that thou mayest observe to do according to all that is written therein, for then thou shalt make thy way prosperous and then thou shalt have good success."* Notice that God didn't say that *He* would make our way prosperous. He clearly stated that we shall make our own way prosperous.

Upon reading this, I asked myself, "Make my way prosperous at what? Have good success at what? Are there only specific things in which I can be prosperous and experience good success? Or is He saying I can prosper at WHATEVER I put my hand to?"

The Psalmist states that we are blessed when we delight (walk according to) the law of the Lord. He denotes that if we meditate in His Law day and night, we shall be like a tree planted by the rivers of water that brings forth his fruit in his season. Our leaf shall not wither; and WHATSOEVER WE DO SHALL PROSPER. Well, there is the answer to my question! I can prosper at WHATEVER I put my hand to.

Not everyone is going to be a Donald Trump (a billionaire real estate investor), with their name splashed across multi-million dollar sky-reaching structures. Not everyone is going to be like Mike (Michael Jordan, a famous basketball player), able to mesmerize crowds with gravity defying game-winning moves. Not everyone is going to be an Oprah Winfrey (a billionaire business woman and talk show hostess) with a philanthropic heart as big as the moon and a bank account to match. Why limit yourself to what someone else has anyway, when you can prosper at whatever you put *your* hand to?

We must consider putting our hand to more things. Whatever our profession—School Teacher, Bus Driver, Custodian, Corporate Executive, Self-Employed Business Owner or Housewife—God promised that if we confess, meditate and observe to do according to His law, we WILL prosper and succeed. Nowhere in the Formula for Success did God say it was contingent upon our job or profession. In fact, our prosperity is unique to us as individuals. We will prosper at the things we enjoy, choose to do and are good at.

I am reminded of the true story about a farmer who followed God's Formula for Success to the letter and naturally became very wealthy. While still humbly maintaining his job as a farmer he bought a plane. His neighbors and friends thought it was absurd and wasteful, but God knew his heart and blessed him accordingly. That farmer eventually retired from farming and went on to span the globe spreading the gospel, building the Kingdom of God.

Generally speaking, the more we understand how a biblical principle works, the more likely we are to practice it. The more we practice it, the more likely we are to not only *understand* how it works, but actually *experience* it working!

So let's read on and explore The Formula for Success, which consists of confession, meditation, and observance to the Word of God. You will soon discover, like I did, how practicing these principles will cause you to prosper and succeed at whatever *you* put *your* hand to.

Chapter One

CONFESSIONS (AFFIRMATIONS) BUILD FAITH

---- ⊕ ----

Foundation Scripture: 2 Corinthians 4:13

"We having the same spirit of faith, according as it is written, I believed, and therefore have I spoken; we also believe, and therefore speak;"

The secular world calls them "affirmations." In the Kingdom of God, they are referred to as "confessions." What are they? In a nutshell, confessions are God's words that when spoken by us in a repetitive fashion produce change.

Years ago, I learned the powerful effect of affirming things from the secular world during a sales meeting. The speaker explained that our destiny could be altered if we repeated our affirmations aloud to ourselves daily. Soon thereafter, I discovered that affirmations derive from the biblical principle of confession, which was given to us by God Himself. Housed within this principle is revelation knowledge of how He designed us to operate on this earth.

We were created to believe what we say—it is that simple. Confessing complies with our communication mechanism. When we believe what we say, we are usually convincing to others and certainly convincing to ourselves. It is not that we have some great truth or fact that others don't have; it is simply that the honesty of our conviction comes through in the things we speak and the forthright manner in which we speak them.

Listeners are drawn to the verbal and nonverbal message that is being communicated: confidence. The listener then either believes the message they are hearing, or they don't. Even in cases where the listener doesn't believe the message, at the very least they are confident that the speaker believes it.

Confessing the scriptures in the Bible keeps us in tune with what God said. God's Word is Truth and He has obligated Himself to carry out His Word. Because we are created to believe what we speak, it is the will of God that we believe and speak what He said in His Word.

A number of things happen when we confess scripture. First, **confessions build faith.** Faith comes by **hearing** the Word of God. From the Greek translation, the New Testament uses the word *hearing* in what is known as *the present active indicative mode*. In other words, our hearing of God's Word takes place in the present tense over and over everyday.

If I desire to receive something from God, all I need to do is find scriptures that deal with what I desire and confess them aloud repeatedly—from the time I awake in the morning, throughout my day, and until I retire at night. Why? Because every time I confess the scriptures to the point where I hear them, my heart believes what it hears me say.

Just thinking about our dreams and desires doesn't give them permission to go anywhere! That's why the Bible tells us we can have what we SAY, not we can have what we think about.

I used to wonder if it really was God's will for me to have the good things the Bible talks about: peace, prosperity, favor, joy, and the list goes on. One day, my Pastor pointed out that God's Word *is* His Will and that every promise in His Word is granted to us. Once I erased the fear, doubt, and disbelief, I knew that all I had to do was confess those things and I would eventually have them.

Please don't misunderstand me; those things that we desire and confess don't usually appear instantly—like "poof" there it is the moment we speak it! In fact, there is no set timetable known to us, which is where faith comes in. We must have faith first to *believe* that we can have what we say and secondly, the faith to *wait* for that which we believe to manifest.

Faith is to the spirit realm what strength is to the physical realm. Just as with energy obtained from food, faith cannot be stored forever. When we eat, we get the energy we need to function and exercise. As we exercise, we build strength. The more we exercise, the greater we grow in our capacity to exercise and get stronger. The stronger we become, the more consistently we need to eat and the cycle continues.

When we confess the scriptures, we expose an energy called faith, which is a combination of belief with action. The more we act on what we believe the greater we increase in our capacity to act on what we believe and the stronger our faith becomes. The stronger our faith becomes the more consistently we need to confess scripture and the cycle continues.

It does not take as much strength to pick up a book and carry it to a desk as it does to pick up a one hundred pound television and carry it to a desk. We must exercise our muscles to build the strength necessary to move the television. The same thing is true with faith. As we continuously confess God's Word, praying and exercising our faith by acting on what we believe, we grow from receiving and moving small things to receiving and moving bigger things. Faith can—and will—move mountains! Therefore, we must be steady and regular with our spiritual nourishment of confessing scriptures.

Jesus said if we have faith as a grain of mustard seed we shall speak to a tree to be plucked up by the root and be planted in the sea and it shall obey us. If we look at faith in terms of quantity, we only need a small amount—as small as a grain of mustard seed. Then we can move trees and mountains.

However, when Jesus rebuked the disciples for having little faith He wasn't talking about *quantity* but their *quality* of faith. I would even venture to say that He referred to their *duration* of faith. If those disciples had absolute confidence in what they believed, enduring until full manifestation would not have been an issue.

As I mentioned before, manifestation is not always immediate. Sometimes it is a process requiring us to keep our faith focused on a thing for an extended period of time in order to "see it through." In other words, don't just believe for a moment. Believe for a month. Believe for a year. Believe for a decade. Believe for however long it takes to receive the answer.

You may think that it is impossible to believe for years or decades for something without giving up halfway through the process. On the contrary, we *do* have the ability to believe that long for something, but only if we use confessions. How so? Well, the more we confess the Word the more we hear it. The more we hear it the more we believe it and act on it. The more we believe it and act on it the more we will continue to confess it.

Repetitive confessing increases the quality of our faith. A higher quality of faith increases our ability to apply our faith for longer periods of time. Throughout this whole process our faith just keeps on building. I am a living testimony that the process works!

Chapter Two

CONFESSIONS
RENEW YOUR MIND

---------------------------- ⊕ ----------------------------

Foundation Scripture: Romans 12:2

"And be not conformed to this world: but be ye transformed by the renewing of your mind, that ye may prove what is that good, and acceptable, and perfect, will of God."

We were created as a three-dimensional being composed of **spirit, soul** and **body**. Our spirit is the most dominant; next is our soul; followed by our body. They act interdependently.

Our **spirit** is the very essence of who we really are. Only through our spirit can we perceive spiritual things and other things we cannot see. It is also the seat of our most accurate understanding. Although we cannot physically see our spirit, our mere existence offers a level of self-realization of its presence.

Our **soul**, otherwise known as the mind, is the place where our will, emotions and intellect reside. It has two command centers: the subconscious mind and the conscious mind.

The **subconscious mind** is the command center that controls 90% of what we do from day to day. It makes up the autopilot mechanism for our learned and instinctive behavior. We don't think about how to walk, drive, or tap our feet. This is all the function of our subconscious mind.

It is through our **conscious mind** that we know what we are thinking from moment to moment. In other words, we are aware of our thoughts. In the conscious mind, our thoughts are filtered through our value system. We determine fact or fantasy and truth or fiction through this system.

Our **value system** is a compilation of the things we believe and is developed by emotional imprints and repetitive hearing. **Emotional imprinting** comes from events that happen in our lives that cause lasting positive or negative emotions. Whether the events are near or far, within our immediate family or our human family, the emotional imprint is the same.

I was a Regional Vice President for a financial services firm for four years, during which time I was given the opportunity to supervise a sales staff. Right away, I noticed there were sales people who were go-getters and sales people who consistently needed to be encouraged.

I wondered why that was, when both groups of people had the capacity to be great producers. Upon investigation, I realized that even though training taught the sales people that they would encounter more "no's" from prospective clients than "yes's," it was the way the word "no" filtered through their value system that determined their level of success.

The people who needed the most encouragement were generally those who, as children, had been negatively imprinted by the word "no." "No" became more than a word—it became associated with emotional or physical pain and a sense of doing or being wrong. For example, when they asked for something and their parents answered with "no," it was said in such a way that hurt the child's feelings. When the child did something wrong, the "no" was followed by a negative consequence that caused short-term physical or long-term emotional pain.[1]

Fear of rejection is the most common plague among non-producing sales people. It registers as an internal feeling of personal rejection when people say "no" to them. They have not learned the difference between someone rejecting what is being offered for sale versus someone rejecting them as a person. Again, this has much to do with how the word "no" filters through their emotional memory. The good news is that the emotional memory is part of the subconscious mind and can be changed through repetitive hearing.

The go-getters, on the other hand, are not discouraged when prospective clients say "no." They just keep making the calls until they find people who will say "yes." This is partly because when they hear the word "no" they understand that people are not rejecting them personally, but are simply rejecting what they are offering."

Emotional events are one way our value system receives information as truth. The other way is through repetitive hearing. **Repetitive hearing** is our internal reinforcement mechanism. It consists of two components: sensory and self-talk.

First, there is a **sensory** component in which repetitive hearing takes place through our environment. We receive messages from our environment through our senses that tells us to accept what we see, hear, touch, taste, and smell as truth. This happens from the cradle to the grave over and over every day. It is as if our environment's voice repeatedly says, "Believe what you continue to see; believe what you continue to hear; believe what you continue to feel or touch; believe what you continue to taste; and believe what you continue to smell."

Secondly, there is **self-talk**. Self-talk is our own inner voice produced from strongholds in our subconscious mind. Studies prove that people, if left to themselves, will follow the loudest and most consistent voice in their lives— their own self-talk. To achieve success, we must learn to manage our self-talk.

Have you ever wondered how a person can desire change and even relocate to a different town, yet they eventually end up with the same scenario that they left behind? Thus the saying, "wherever you go, there you are." Well, that's the result of untrained, negative self-talk. Like looking in a mirror, recurring circumstances reflect our patterns of thought and the strongholds they form.

Patterns of thought are higher forms of thought that have voice. They run on a pattern in our subconscious mind similar to how an operating system runs on a computer. Every time thoughts complete their pattern they speak in the form of self-talk. This self-talk bombards our conscious mind to be reinforced as truth to our value system. Patterns of thought form **strongholds**, which could be positive or negative. Strongholds are merely reinforced patterns of thought, barriers formed around our thinking, if you will, to protect that way of thinking.

As human beings, we are incapable of originating thoughts in our conscious mind. However, we are receivers who receive thoughts transmitted from God directly through our spirit. Unfortunately, though, we can just as easily receive thoughts from the devil—through the world's system in the form of our environment and carnal suggestions—as well as through our own existing patterns of thought and strongholds.

God wants us to pull down these strongholds by renewing our mind. For as a man thinks in his heart, so is he.

Self-talk in our conscious mind reveals who we really are. Why? Well, because eventually we believe what we hear ourselves say and therefore we begin to obey our own words. However, through renewing our mind we can pull down every stronghold and barrier which limits our thoughts. We can only go as far as we think we can. When we change our thoughts, we transform ourselves to reveal our infinite ability.

So how do we renew our minds? We renew our minds by confessing the Word of God. The Word of God sanctifies us and the Word of God cleanses us.

When we repeatedly confess the Word of God, our confessions override our self-talk. The more we hear the Word the more faith is produced because faith comes by hearing the Word of God. Every time faith is produced our value system is being reprogrammed. Simultaneously, as the power of God's Word cuts down strongholds, a new pattern of thought is established through self-talk and opens us to the infinite possibilities of success. It is a total system override and overhaul!

We are changed from the inside out. Our patterns of thought change, our values change, our attitudes change, our actions change and our circumstances change. Primarily, our self-talk changes and we become sanctified.

In the physical realm, we are set apart in two ways: by our conduct and by our prosperity. When the world sees us, they will want to be like us because we will truly be a changed people. Then more souls will be drawn to the Kingdom of God.

Suppose you were in a large group of people who drove dirty old cars to a seminar. At this seminar, the motivating speaker informed the group that they had a choice to either leave the meeting in a new, free, clean car, or leave in the same dirty old car that brought them there.

Which car would you choose? Which one do you think the entire group would choose? It's obvious: the clean new car—for free! We will look oh so impressive in our new cars!

That is how it is going to be when the world sees us healed, prosperous, filled with the joy of the Lord and of clean character! We won't need to "sell them" on the benefits of receiving Jesus Christ as their Lord and Savior when our positive lifestyle is an advertising billboard for them. They will approach us with a desire to be saved because this move of God sells itself.

Now, the real test of self-talk comes into play when we check in with that group of new car owners several months later. How many of them would you guess have allowed those new shiny cars to become dirty and old looking? We all know way too many people who would fall into this category. Again, our self-talk must change by becoming changed from the inside out.

When we consider it from this point of view, confessing the Word becomes our duty. Changing from the inside out becomes our mission and living like Heaven on Earth becomes our reward.

Chapter Three

CONFESSIONS CALL
FORTH THINGS

---⊕---

Foundation Scripture: Genesis 1:1,11-12

"In the beginning God created the heaven and the earth. And God said, Let the earth bring forth grass, the herb yielding seed, and the fruit tree yielding fruit after his kind, whose seed is in itself, upon the earth: and it was so. And the earth brought forth grass, and herb yielding seed after his kind, and the tree yielding fruit, whose seed was in itself, after his kind: and God saw that it was good."

In the beginning, God created everything by using the Word to call it forth. *All things were made by the Word, and without the Word was not anything made that were made. Nothing existed before the Word; nothing exists without the Word; and by the Word all things are held together.*

God also used the Word to call forth things out of their source. When He created grass, herbs, plants and trees, He spoke to the earth and the earth brought forth. When He created the sun and the moon, He spoke to the heavens. When He created the fish in the sea and the fowl of the air, He spoke to the waters.

When He created the animals and insects, He spoke to the earth. However, when God created mankind, He spoke to *Himself.* God always spoke before He acted. Before He formed mankind He used the Word to call mankind forth out of the source of mankind, which is God Himself.

Out of all God's creation mankind is the only one that He personally shaped and formed. God shaped man in His own image and after His own likeness. God then gave man the duty of dominion. Everything was made to produce after its own kind. So when God made man, He made us to resemble and imitate Him.

One of the ways God operates is to use His Word to create—to call things forth, hold things together and keep things in their place. Just think; we were created to perform the same way! For example, just as an earthly king manages his kingdom using his words, we must also learn to walk in our kingly way.

The king has dominion over everything within his rule. If the king calls forth something, his servants bring it. Kings, themselves, do not transport items. Nor do they clean or cook. A king even has servants to bath him so he does not have to wash himself. Everything is accomplished by his words.

The Kingdom of God works the same way. When God created everything, everything was created to obey His Word. Whatever does not have the ability to carry out its own obedience, the angels have the task of causing things to conform. It is important to note that angels play a major role in delivering messages to us from the Father and carrying out the requests of His Word. In other words, the angels serve God by serving us.

They serve us because we are children of God, heirs of salvation and joint heirs with Christ. Therefore, we are a royal priesthood. We are royalty and have been given authority by the King. That is why we were instructed to say and do everything in the name and authority of the Lord Jesus Christ. We are an extension of His authority. However, just having authority is not enough. We must understand how to affect the authority we have been given.

Angels do not obey everything *we* say, but they do obey every word of God. In fact, the Book of Psalms tells us that the angels excel in strength. They bless the Lord by doing His commandments and by obeying the voice of His word.

In essence, angels obey the voice of God's Word. Who gives the Word voice? We do, when we confess the Word. I personally experienced the obedience of angels when I confess Isaiah 54:13 (Amplified Version) every morning: *"And all your [spiritual] children shall be disciples [taught by the Lord and obedient to His will], and great shall be the peace and undisturbed composure of your children."*

One day, I got a call from a police officer that my family had been in a car accident. A driver fell asleep at the wheel and went through a red light and hit the side of the SUV carrying my wife and children. My family's vehicle was traveling about 35 mph through the green light, while the vehicle with the sleeping driver went through the red light going about 45 mph. They collided in the center of the intersection and the impact could be heard for blocks. Our SUV ended up on the curb in front of a convenience store.

I was a Deputy Sheriff at the time and immediately sped to the scene. Upon arriving, I was allowed through the crowd. The police and paramedics who were already there said we witnessed a complete miracle, as my wife and children did not sustain any injuries! There was just a dent in the side of our SUV. The car that hit them was completely totaled and the man received medical attention by the paramedics.

Of course, there were some doubting people who stated that the accident should've never happened if angels were truly protecting my family. But I beg to differ! It was because the angels obeyed the voice of God's word that the accident wasn't worse. Who gave God's Word voice? I did, when I prayed and confessed, *"Great is the peace and undisturbed composure of my children."*

We can use the Word of God to call forth anything—whether it is healing, joy, wisdom, or money. Whatever we call forth, if it cannot move itself, the angels can cause it to manifest; as long as we use the Word of God to call it forth. When it manifests, it will stay manifested so long as we continue to believe the Word we confessed.

In the Word, there is power to create, power to bring forth what is created, and power to hold things in their place once they are brought forth. That power is affected by our confession!

Chapter Four

MEDITATION

Foundation Scripture: Psalm 5:1

"Give ear to my words, O LORD, consider my meditation."

Remember this formula for success: *"Confess the Word of God, meditate in it day and night that you may observe to do all that is written therein."* So far, we covered how confessions build faith, renew the mind and call forth things. That now brings us to the subject of meditation.

Meditation in one word is powerful! An easy way to understand the power of meditation is to understand how reading works. Reading and meditation share some of the same processes.

When we read, we self-talk. That leads our conscious mind to create images of the words we say to ourselves. Comprehension takes place and is then filtered through our value system to be assessed as truth or untruth. That is why we generally believe what we read—especially if the information does not conflict with our value system. Remember, we were created to believe what we say. So when we read we self-talk and then we believe what we hear ourselves say.

When we meditate, we also create lasting mental images from visualization and self-talk. The visualization could be images of words, pictures, sounds and/ or feelings. When we visualize, we project the images in our minds as if they were actually happening. This is done repetitively. Thus, meditation involves repetitive visualization and self-talk, which can then lead to illumination.

Illumination is spiritual insight—also known as revelation—which if acted upon will cause acceleration in achievement. It will also cause the renewing of our mind and the building of our faith. The good thing about this process is that it is a law, which means it is guaranteed to work for us if we do it. The bad thing about this process is that it is a law. I have seen people meditate on that which is detrimental to others and accelerate in the achievement of evil things.

Sometimes, I use a juicer in the morning to make <u>fresh</u> fruit and vegetable juice for my breakfast. In order to make the juice, I cut up the fruit and vegetables, put them in the juicer and then use a pusher to put pressure on them against the grinding blade which extracts the juice. Let's apply that same concept to illumination to understand what happens to the Word of God when we meditate it. We put the scriptures into our minds one piece at a time by memorizing them. We then put pressure on the Word through repetitive visualization and self-talk (meditation) which finally extracts revelation.

When we meditate on the Word of God long enough the Word has a voice in and of Himself. In time, that voice will speak to us—whether audible or as an unction in our spirit. That is why I believe the answers to ANY problem on earth—whether it is related to family, faith, finances, health, business challenges or anything else—can be discovered using the powerful combination of confessing and meditating God's Word.

Confessing and meditating God's Word puts us in agreement with what God said and therefore pleases God. Confessing and mediating God's Word also produces change in our attitude and behavior and empowers us to "observe to do" that which He said.

The ability to "observe to do" is more commonly known as obedience. Obedience is the final step in the Formula for Success.

Chapter Five

OBEDIENCE
(OBSERVE TO DO)
CAUSES BLESSINGS TO FLOW

---⊕---

Foundation Scripture: Deuteronomy 28:13

"And the LORD shall make thee the head, and not the tail; and thou shalt be above only, and thou shalt not be beneath; if that thou hearken unto the commandments of the LORD thy God, which I command thee this day, to observe and to do them."

It is important to **observe to do—to obey**—what the Word of God says. Obedience to God's Word creates an "alignment" that **causes blessings to flow**, **sends protection our way** and **activates our spiritual power**.

Rivers have water currents that flow downward. When boats travel upstream, their engines have to work harder because they are traveling against the current. If the boat is traveling with the current, its engines can sometimes even take a break while the boat continues to travel almost effortlessly. Blessings operate like rivers and obedience is what causes those blessings to flow.

In the beginning was the Word, the Word was with God, and the Word was God.
The Word of God created all things and the Word holds all things together. The Word
holds things together because its power flows directly from God through His
Word. It flows downward through us for the things that are to be held together.

Like a river that begins its journey from its upstream origin and then surges
downward to the low lands of the delta—where it deposits the riches it collected
along the way—so is the Word of God. That powerful and sanctified Word
loaded with riches flows to us from on high like a mighty river. When we travel
with its current, we are rewarded along the way and gain spiritual, mental,
physical and yes, material bounty in the delta of our lives.

When we don't obey God's Word, our lives are difficult and full of struggle
(That is why Proverbs 13:15 says that *"the way of transgressors is hard"*) because
we are attempting to travel against the current. However, when we *do* obey His
commandments, then peace, prosperity, wholeness, rest, health, safety, happiness
and His favor in our lives will flow as the river. Our righteousness will flow like
the waves of the sea as the blessings of God overtake us.

Notice that the scriptures never advise us to seek the blessings. No, the
Word commands us to seek the Lord *only* and obey His Word. When we do
this, the blessings will automatically catch up to us in the current and positively
engulf us.

Chapter Six

OBEDIENCE PROTECTS US

---------------- ⊕ ----------------

Foundation Scripture: Ephesians 6:16

"Above all, taking the shield of faith, wherewith ye shall be able to quench all the fiery darts of the wicked."

Faith can be defined as "Belief in what God has said and then acting upon that which was said." Faith is a spiritual force; not an earthly or fleshly one. It is not limited to belief in what we think with our limited, natural minds or belief in what we have seen or experienced in our finite capacities. Faith is belief that the Word of God is truth, based on who originally spoke The Word—God Himself.

Faith is full confidence that God cannot lie. Whatsoever He tells us we are to first speak it; secondly, receive it as truth; and lastly and most importantly act on it. Faith (belief in what God has said) must be accompanied by action in order for it to work in our lives. If action is missing then faith cannot work. It is that simple.

We act on what we believe by observing to do what we say or confess. (Remember, "Confession" is to say what God has said.) We were made to speak what we believe and to believe what we speak. So again, I cannot stress enough that we need to understand that when we hear or read God's Word, we should say it, receive it as truth and then act on it. This is Faith!

Now, the phrase "taking the shield of faith" means that faith is also meant to protect us. It is when we say what God has said, receive it as truth, speak what we believe and then obey what we speak that our belief becomes the faith that protect us.

Faith and obedience are synonymous. Though they do not share the same meaning every time, it is a fact that obedience to God's Word does not exist without faith and faith does not exist without obedience to God's Word. The Bible says, *"Show me your faith without deeds, and I will show you my faith by what I do."* James 2:18 (NIV)

Thus the quote, "I would rather see a sermon than hear one any day." James was saying that it is impossible for faith to exist without obedience or actions that are consistent with what we say we believe.

Remember in Chapter Five we learned that the power of God flows through His Word like a current in a river. Well, Isaiah tells us that if we obey God's commandments then our **peace** will also flow as a river and our **righteousness** as the waves of the sea.

The word peace is translated from the Hebrew word that means "wholeness" by way of prosperity, health, happiness, rest, favor, wellness, and safety (protection). So when we confess God's Word and observe to do what we confess, **safety and protection** becomes a constant in our lives.

There is another scripture that is important to take note of: James 4:7. We hear it partially quoted many times as *"Resist the devil and he will flee."* But that is not where the victory lies in that verse. The victory is in *"<u>Submit yourselves therefore to God</u>, resist the devil, and he will flee from you."* God wants us to see that our protection is in our submission and obedience to His Will; which is His Word.

One of my favorite verses is 2 Corinthians 10:3-6. In it Paul writes, *"Though we walk in the flesh, we do not war after the flesh. For the weapons of our warfare are not carnal but mighty through God to the pulling down of Strongholds, casting down imaginations, and every high thing that exalts itself against the knowledge of*

God and bringing into captivity every thought to the obedience of Christ; and having in a readiness to revenge all disobedience, when your obedience is fulfilled.

The revelation in this verse is that some of our greatest battles are fought in our thought life and the thought life of those we lead and serve. We are empowered to pull down negative patterns of thinking (negative strongholds), imaginations and every high thing that exalts itself against the deliverance and liberation that the knowledge of God brings. The empowerment to do this is in our obedience.

The "high things" mentioned in this scripture refer to spiritual barriers—high walls, if you will—that hinder progress in people's lives. Obedience ignites faith. In that same way, pride, unforgiveness, stinginess and the like empower these spiritual barriers. High things produce unwillingness in the heart to change.

The phrase, "Having in a readiness to revenge all disobedience," means that everything under our authority will come to order. That is our church if we are the leader; our household if we are the head; our finances; and everything else in our life. It will all come to order when we are obedient first.

Obedience protects us from hindrances in our lives. It protects us from disorder and empowers us to be victorious in spiritual warfare. Obedience causes us to dwell in safety and to shield ourselves from the fiery darts of the evil one. Obedience protects us from our own thoughts that are sometimes ungodly. Overall, obedience activates our spiritual power!

Chapter Seven

Obedience Activates Our Spiritual Power and Authority

---------------------- ⊕ ----------------------

Foundation Scripture: Matthew 8:8-10

"The centurion answered and said, Lord, I am not worthy that thou shouldest come under my roof: but speak the word only, and my servant shall be healed. For I am a man under authority, having soldiers under me: and I say to this man, Go, and he goeth; and to another, Come, and he cometh; and to my servant, Do this, and he doeth it. When Jesus heard it, he marveled and said to them that followed, Verily I say unto you, I have not found so great faith, no, not in Israel."

All power operates by **submission or obedience to authority**.

By now, we have established the fact that words govern everything. For instance, when people are placed in positions of power no one physically lifts them up and places them on a high seat of some sort. Instead, it is all done by words. With words a king can place a person in a position of great power and authority and with words the one given the authority exercises it.

The same is true in the Kingdom of God. All power in Heaven and Earth was given to Christ Jesus. This is very important to know because Christ Jesus is the Head of every believer in Christ. So whatever power and authority rests on Christ rests on the believer in Christ as well. Isn't that good news?

However, just because we have that power and authority doesn't necessarily mean it's working on our behalf. In fact, until we make the choice to activate this spiritual power it lies dormant. Spiritual power and authority—like natural power and authority—is a force that flows when obedience, submission and boldness (to carry out the mission of the higher authority) are engaged.

When the Centurion in Matthew 8:8-10 said, *"I am a man under authority, having soldiers under me…"* He was saying that he understood how it all worked. The Centurion was obedient to the spoken and written word of his government. He was submissive to the person over him who represented his government and he had boldness to carry out the mission of his government. Power and authority flowed through him in such a way that every time he gave an order his soldiers carried it out.

The Centurion's remark to Jesus was so on target that Jesus marveled. Until that time, Jesus had not found anyone who understood that the truths that govern how things operate in our natural realm (that which we *can* see) are the same truths that govern how things operate in the spirit realm (that which we *cannot* see). For all truth is parallel. The Centurion understood it, believed it and acted upon it in order to obtain healing for his servant through the words Jesus spoke.

Spiritual power and authority has already been granted to us. Yet, it requires our obedience to God's Word—both written and spoken—in order for that spiritual power to be activated. Our prosperity, healing, miracles, etc. does not obey us unless we are in alignment first by obeying God.

In John 15, Jesus said, *"If you abide in me and my words abide in you, you shall ask what you will and it shall be done unto you. For without me, you can do nothing."* Herein lays the secret to obedience and how to exercise spiritual power. First, the Lord's words must abide in us, which means we must confess and meditate them in order to obey them. Secondly, we must ask for what we will or desire.

Words are the key to everything! It is through words that we exercise our spiritual power. How else will divine assistance, salvation of souls, healings, wisdom, words of knowledge and victories in business deals happen even though the odds are against us? We have to first ask for them!

I really like the fact that we must ask for what we desire. It lets us know that we are not the ones doing the work. We speak the words; the Father in Heaven does the work. This is important because it keeps us from being prideful, thinking that *we* are doing the work when it is the Lord who does the work. To *Him* belongs all the glory!

In Job 22:21-28, Job caught a glimpse of the spiritual power and authority that comes from obedience to God's Word. *"Acquaint now thyself with him, and be at peace: thereby good shall come unto thee. Receive, I pray thee, the law from his mouth, and lay up his words in thine heart. If thou return to the Almighty, thou shalt be built up, thou shalt put away iniquity far from thy tabernacles. Then shalt thou lay up gold as dust, and the gold of Ophir as the stones of the brooks. Yea, the Almighty shall be thy defense, and thou shalt have plenty of silver. For then shalt thou have thy delight in the Almighty, and shalt lift up thy face unto God. Thou shalt make thy prayer unto him, and he shall hear thee, and thou shalt pay thy vows. Thou shalt also decree a thing, and it shall be established unto thee: and the light shall shine upon thy ways."*

Job was saying for us to familiarize ourselves with God and get to know Him intimately. Conduct ourselves in such a way as to be able to look Him in the eye with a clear conscious. If we meditate His words in our heart and willingly obey them, we shall increase. We shall also put away wickedness and injustice far from our bodies and places of worship.

When we do this, then God shall be our defender and we shall have plenty of money. Our adoration and affection shall be in the Almighty and we shall look to Him for guidance and provision. We shall ask Him for our desires and He shall hear. We shall then do what we promised Him we would do. We shall also decree (speak or command) a thing and it shall be done for us. Then it will be easier to understand and do that which we desire to accomplish.

Once our spiritual power is activated by our obedience and we confess the Word calling forth things, then "things" shall manifest. We can call forth healing and it will manifest. We can call forth joy and it will manifest. We can call forth wholeness and restoration and it will manifest. We can call forth money and opportunity and it will manifest.

The formula for success is confession, meditation and observation of what the Word says to do. This is the basic foundation that every believer should practice daily. This is the formula that will keep us in line with God's will. As long as we remain in His will we experience good success.

In my first thirty days of practicing it, there was a noticeable difference in my life. Within ninety days, my thinking dramatically changed. Within one year's time, my life totally transformed in every area—especially my income. My income was five times higher than my previous year's income with less time spent working!

Now that we have the basic foundation of the Formula for Success let us build on it by gaining an understanding of the only three principles in the Bible that the Lord says He will command the blessing upon. Let's get ready for wealth beyond our imagination!

Part I – Action Points

All increase begins with the Word of God. Mark 4:14 says, "The Sower sows the Word." Another way to say it is, "The Planter plants the Word." The Word of God is the seed that will eventually grow into a tree within our hearts and the fruits of that tree are the actions and results we see in our everyday lives.

Jesus said, "Every tree shall be known by their fruits."

Ye shall know them by their fruits. Do men gather grapes of thorns, or figs of thistles? Even so every good tree brings forth good fruit; but a corrupt tree brings forth evil fruit. A good tree cannot bring forth evil fruit; neither *can* a corrupt tree bring forth good fruit. Every tree that doesn't bring forth good fruit is hewn down, and cast into the fire.

Wherefore by their fruits ye shall know them. Matthew 7:16-20

Psalm 1 explains how to become a good tree bearing good fruit.

Blessed *is* the man that doesn't walk in the counsel of the ungodly (Don't do what ungodly people advise you to do), nor stands in the way of sinners (don't go and commit acts of sin with sinners), nor sits in the seat of the scornful (don't talk negatively about people nor treat them as if you are superior to them.) But his delight *is* in the law of the LORD; and in his law doth he meditate day and night. And he shall be like a tree planted by the rivers of water, that brings forth his fruit in his season; his leaf also shall not wither; and whatsoever he doeth shall prosper. Psalm 1:1-3

If we meditate on the Word of God day and night, then the Word of God will lead us to a place where we would flourish.

1. What are you believing God for? (Write it in the most specific, simplest and briefest 1 – 2 sentence(s) as possible.)

_____

_____

_____

_____

_____

2. What scripture(s) will you confess and meditate to build your faith, renew your mind and call forth things?

_____

_____

_____

_____

_____

3. What insights and ideas come to mind as a result of your scripture meditation in the morning and evening?

_____

_____

_____

_____

_____

4. What steps have you taken to implement the ideas from question number 3?

_____

_____

_____

_____

_____

Additional Notes

PRINCIPLE OF SOWING

Principle #1
The Principle of Sowing

---⊕---

Foundation Scripture Leviticus 25:18-22

"Wherefore ye shall do my statutes, and keep my judgments, and do them; and ye shall dwell in the land in safety. And the land shall yield her fruit, and ye shall eat your fill, and dwell therein in safety. And if ye shall say, "What shall we eat the seventh year? Behold, we shall not sow, nor gather in our increase:" Then I will command my blessing upon you in the sixth year, and it shall bring forth fruit for three years. And ye shall sow the eighth year, and eat yet of old fruit until the ninth year; until her fruits come in ye shall eat of the old store."

This scripture is a classic example of the fact that there is a spiritual root to increase. If the root is evil, then the increase is accompanied by sorrow. If the root is good, then the increase has no sorrow with it. Obedience to God's Word makes the spiritual root of increase a good one. It is the blessing of the Lord that makes us rich and adds no sorrow with it.

Another truth to observe is that God does not always follow what makes sense to us. Most farmers would agree that it does not make sense to think that land that produces only one year's worth of crop, would all of a sudden on every sixth year, produce enough for three years. Obedience to God's Word does not follow what makes sense, therefore, it takes faith to obey and follow God. There is no way to know if the land would produce enough for three years other than to take God at His Word.

It is this mentality of believing God that we should adopt. Faith is not a feeling, nor does it always make sense. We must believe and follow God's Word despite our feelings, despite what others may think and despite potential ridicule. In doing so, we can use the following principles to multiply our income, multiply our savings, multiply our opportunities, as well as increase our health and peace.

There are three principles upon which God said that He would command the Blessing. They are: "the Principle of Sowing," "the Principle of Saving," and "the Principle of Agreement." There are places in scripture that speak about blessings that are bestowed upon us without us doing anything to cause it. However, these three principles depend on us to activate them and reap their benefits.

My pastor was a fighter jet pilot during the Vietnam War. He often talks about the laws of flight, specifically the Law of Gravity, the Law of Drag, the Law of Thrust and the Law of Lift. Air is a physical substance that has weight. If you are lighter than air you will fly, if you are heavier than air you will fall to the ground. Why? Because the Law of Gravity attracts you to the earth's core.

The Law of Drag always shows up in the form of resistance. It is caused when the air (a physical substance that has weight) moves across the surface of the airplane and creates friction which causes the airplanes to slow down. So, in order to overcome the Law of Gravity and the Law of Drag, the Law of Thrust is needed.

The Law of Thrust is the force that propels the airplane forward. Thrust is provided by the airplane's propulsion mechanism which is usually a jet engine or a propeller. When the Law of Thrust propels the airplane forward with enough force to overcome the Law of Drag, the airplane will accelerate. The air flowing over the wings creates low pressure while the air flowing under the wings creates high pressure and causes the airplane to benefit from the Law of Lift.

The Law of Lift happens when the high pressure under the airplane and the low pressure over the plane overcome the weight of the plane enabling it to lift and fly. The gist of it all is, if the thrust is greater than the drag, the airplane will accelerate forward, and if the lift is greater than the weight of the airplane (caused by gravity), the airplane will climb and fly.

It is a law whether we believe it or not. It works every time it is properly engaged whether we have knowledge of it or not. The three principles where God said that He would command the Blessing upon are the same way. They are laws that will work 100% of the time if we would properly engage them.

In order to understand the Principle of Sowing, we would do well to observe it through the eyes of a farmer. Every farmer knows that "sowing" is the key to harvest. The soil may need to be watered from time to time as well, but without sowing seed the farmer has nothing of value to expect in return. In order to maximize the benefits of this principle, there are two foundational methods of sowing that we must know through practice in order for the principle to work, and they are: Tithes and Offerings.

Chapter Eight

PAY THE TITHE

---⊕---

Foundation Scripture: Malachi 3:10

"Bring the whole tithe into the storehouse, that there may be food in my house..." Malachi 3:10

Ken was a farmer who owned vast acres of land and employed hundreds of workers to help him develop it. One afternoon, one of his sons asked if he could go into business for himself by taking a few acres of land to sow and reap for a profit. Ken happily granted his son more land than what he asked for and even blessed him with servants to assist him. The only requirement was that his son would have to pay a tithe (ten percent) of his increase to his dad, and the son could keep the other ninety percent.

After a while, the son discovered that as he obeyed his father by paying the tithe, he continued to increase. Within a few years, he went from paying his dad $10,000 and keeping $90,000 for himself, to paying his dad $100,000 and keeping $900,000 for himself. However, as he continued to increase, he soon began to feel that the ten percent that he paid his father was too much money. So he started to withhold more than he should.

Do you think the son had a right to decide whether or not he should pay his dad the entire ten percent? Of course not, because his father owned all the land in the first place!

In the same sense, God owns everything. God owns the planet we live on, and the air we breathe. He owns the jobs we have and the income we earn from those jobs. Should we think it strange that He asks us to pay ten percent of what is His in the first place?

Let's look at various scriptures that support tithing...

"Even from the days of your fathers ye are gone away from mine ordinances, and have not kept them. Return unto me, and I will return unto you, saith the LORD of hosts. But ye said, Wherein shall we return? Will a man rob God? Yet ye have robbed me. But ye say, Wherein have we robbed thee? In tithes and offerings." Malachi 3:7-8

After stating that the descendants of Jacob had <u>turned away</u> from His decrees, the Lord commanded them to <u>re-turn </u>to Him. How were they to <u>re-turn</u>? Very simply, they were to return to Him by not denying Him Tithes and Offerings.

God said, *"Stop robbing God!"*

Can Man rob God? We might think that it is impossible to rob God, but it isn't.

To "steal," means to take what belongs to another without their consent and without their knowledge. To "rob," means to take what belongs to another by threat or force. In other words, when we take what belongs to another by force, we are taking directly from that person; they know we are taking it, yet they are limited in their ability to stop us.

When God created man in His own image, He created in us the ability to make choices. When He communicates with us, He does so in a way that is not forceful, but allows us to choose what we would do. It is also interesting to note that God does not cross that line He created by violating the choices we make. Therefore, we *are* robbing God when we don't pay our tithes.

The first tenth of everything we have gained by the grace and favor of God belongs to God. It is holy unto Him. Therefore, when we make the decision to withhold the tithe, we are forcefully taking what rightfully belongs to God.

He knows what we are doing, but He granted us the ability to choose and has therefore limited Himself in His ability to stop us.

With the ability to choose, comes the responsibility of making choices. The one who makes the choice bears the consequence of that choice—good or bad. Sometimes those consequences are dire. Thus the proverb, "The curse causeless shall not come." If we see that our finances are cursed, it is because there is a cause. Or more specifically, a choice we have made to produce the cause.

"Ye are cursed with a curse: for ye have robbed me, even this whole nation. Bring ye all the tithes into the storehouse, that there may be meat in mine house, and prove me now herewith, saith the LORD of hosts, if I will not open you the windows of heaven, and pour you out a blessing, that there shall not be room enough to receive it. And I will rebuke the devourer for your sakes, and he shall not destroy the fruits of your ground; neither shall your vine cast her fruit before the time in the field, saith the LORD of hosts. And all nations shall call you blessed: for ye shall be a delightful land, saith the LORD of hosts." Malachi 3:9-12

God judges all of our choices. He rewards and punishes accordingly; delivers blessings and curses where applicable. That is why He says, *"You are under a curse."* Because He put a whole system into place that will give us the applicable consequence to our choices.

Imagine a sphere with a line down the center of it. On one side of the line are blessings and on the other side are curses. The side with blessings is full of light and the side with curses is full of darkness. There is no middle ground!

When we choose to obey the Word of God, we spiritually walk in the light where the good consequences are—blessings. When we choose *not* to obey God's Word, we spiritually turn ourselves around and walk over the line into darkness where the negative consequences are—curses. God wants us to re-turn ourselves around to walk on the side full of light and blessings by paying our tithes and offerings.

Now imagine putting this principle to the test. God commanded us to bring the tithes (that which is rightfully His) to the place He has designated (the storehouse – the place where we gather for worship and receive spiritual food) that there might be provisions in His house. He says to test Him in this! He would bless us so much that we will be overwhelmed with blessings. He would take away those things that prevent us from getting ahead. Our blessings will be so great that others will see us and call us blessed. God not only wants what is rightfully His to be a blessing to others; He wants us to receive the blessings that come by obeying His word.

What's sad is that even with the knowledge of what we have just read, there are still some people who will say that tithing is for the Old Testament only. They would argue that it is not in the New Testament and therefore does not apply to us. How can they say that? Of course it's in the New Testament and does apply to us! Look at what Jesus says in Matthew 23:23:

> *"Woe unto you, scribes and Pharisees, hypocrites! for ye pay tithe of mint and anise and cummin, and have omitted the weightier matters of the law, judgment, mercy, and faith: these ought ye to have done, and not to leave the other undone."* (KJV)

> *"Woe to you, teachers of the law and Pharisees, you hypocrites! You give a tenth of your spices--mint, dill and cummin. But you have neglected the more important matters of the law--justice, mercy and faithfulness. You should have practiced the latter, without neglecting the former."* (NIV)

Jesus said that the Pharisees tithed on everything from the greatest to the least, but neglected the more important matters of the law: justice, mercy and faithfulness. He said that they should practice justice, mercy, and faithfulness, without neglecting to practice tithing.

Payment of tithes is not physically forced; but it is not a matter of conscience before the Lord either. If paying tithes were an option, there would be no penalty for not paying them. The fact that not paying tithes invokes a curse on the non-tithing Christian is a clear indication of how strongly God feels about tithing.

We cannot expect to get wealth God's way without tithing! To grasp an understanding of this, pay close attention to the terminology used in this next scripture:

> *"Bring the whole tithe into the storehouse, that there may be food in my house. Test me in this," says the LORD Almighty, "and see if I will not throw open the floodgates of heaven and pour out so much blessing that you will not have room enough for it. I will prevent pests from devouring your crops, and the vines in your fields will not cast*

their fruit," says the LORD Almighty. "Then all the nations will call you blessed, for yours will be a delightful land," says the LORD Almighty. Malachi 3:10-12 (NIV)

This passage of scripture is the only scripture in the entire Bible that instructs us to test the Lord. If the believer will test the Lord by tithing, this scripture says that the Lord will **throw open** the **floodgates** of heaven and **pour out so much blessing** that we won't have enough room to take it all in.

In addition to that, the Lord will rebuke the devourer (destroyer) of our crops (our harvest) and our vines will not drop their fruit before its time (our plans would come to fruition at the ideal time). And if that wasn't enough, God said that He would bless us so good that others will be able to notice it and call us blessed. All of these good things are ours if we obey the Lord in our tithing. Isn't God good?

Tithing must be the foundation of every believer's wealth building plan. Without tithing, the windows of heaven will not be open. Even if we have no desire to get wealthy and just want to live modestly, we still must tithe. In so doing, we serve The Lord and we help others. It's that simple: if we tithe, we will receive blessings, and if we rob God, we will receive curses. There is no middle ground!

Paying tithes is not the same as sowing. In fact, we are not sowing until we purpose in our heart to give offerings over and above our tithes. Giving offerings, as the next chapter covers, would then be our first level of sowing.

Chapter Nine

OFFERINGS

---⊕---

Foundation Scripture: 2 Corinthians 9:7

"...for God loves a cheerful giver."

As we learned in Chapter Eight, paying tithes is the basics; the foundation of financial stewardship. Giving offerings after we have paid tithes is the next level. Giving is an expression of love, an expression of thanks, a manifestation of our fellowship, and a way to worship and honor the Lord with our substance.

When we love someone, then what is important to them becomes important to us because love is sharing. When we love someone, we share their joys and their sorrows. We share their plans and their goals. We share their victories and their defeats.

It is because of God's love for us that He gave His only begotten Son to die for our sins. It is also because of His love that we wake up in our right minds, and have food to eat, clothes to put on, a job to go to and healthy bodies to work with. He loves us enough to talk with us and desires us to talk with Him. He really cares about how we feel and how we are maturing in Christ. Everything He does for us and gives to us is for our benefit and the benefit of those whose lives we touch.

It is this great example of giving out of love for others that we are to follow. The fruit produced from this kind of love ought to be our motivation for giving offerings.

When we think of offerings in this present day, we usually think of money given to the church in addition to the tithe. I must admit that until I did the research for this book, I thought the same thing. However, I have found that there is a much deeper meaning behind giving offerings.

In the Old Testament, offerings fell into three broad types. The **guilt and sin offerings** were offered first, covering the sin of the people. This had to take place first. Next, the **burnt offerings** expressed complete dedication to God. Ultimately, the **fellowship offering** expressed fellowship with God.

These first three were mandatory; whereas, a forth type, the freewill offerings, was done by choice, and always in addition to the other offerings. The fellowship and freewill offerings were not offered in order to obtain fellowship with God. They were offered because fellowship with God existed.

From the Old Testament to the New Testament, nothing regarding offerings has changed. Our sinful nature was not a matter of choice but rather how we were born. We were born into sin and condemned to death from birth because of our sinful nature. But God so loved the world that He gave His only begotten Son, Jesus Christ, to be the Atoning Sacrifice for our sin, settling our debt to God and restoring our peace with God.

Peace is a necessary part of any relationship. When God created us with the ability to choose, He gave us a choice of who we would submit our will to and fellowship with. His desire was that we would choose to fellowship with and be at peace with Him. It is important to understand that once peace is restored, fellowship has to be affected and relationship has to be developed.

For the sake of our relationship with God, we are responsible for our offerings of dedication and fellowship. We ought to be totally dedicated to God in our body and mind for that is our living sacrifice. For this cause, it is also important not to neglect our fellowship and freewill offerings which are our giving of our time (to serve) and money (a gift that is in addition to the tithe.)

Naturally, fellowship is never one-sided. It takes two to tango. Therefore, our part in this fellowship encompasses:

- **Our love for God;** hence, our fellow man.
- **Devotion of our time** to worship and to commune with God.
- **Giving of our time and resources** to provide for the growth and provision of the Kingdom of God.

If we take a moment to understand our role in the plan of God to save those who are lost, we would see how He reaches out to lost souls through the love of Christians. He also matures believers through the love of other mature believers—through giving.

Let us look at First Corinthians Chapter 13 in the King James' version to see what is said about the word love:

"And now abideth faith, hope, charity, these three; but the greatest of these is charity." 1Corinthians 13:13

I wondered for years, why did the King James' version substitute the word "charity" for the Greek word "agape." "Agape" is the word from which we translate: unconditional love.

The word charity means: the unconditional, benevolent, freewill giving of one's self, time and/or substance to fulfill the needs of another, from whom there is no expectation of repayment. In fact, Webster's College Dictionary defined charity as: Christian love, i.e. agape.

After much thought, I realized that love really isn't love unless it is expressed in action. In other words, if you really want to know if someone loves you unconditionally, look for the things they have done to benefit you without expecting repayment. That is the true sign of love; for love is not love unless it is expressed in action.

The following are a few verses that tie together giving and God's love....

"Beloved, if God so loved us, we ought also to love one another. Hereby perceive we the love of God, because he laid down his life for us: and we ought to lay down our lives for the brethren. But whoso hath this world's good, and seeth his brother

have need, and shutteth up his bowels of compassion from him, how dwelleth the love of God in him? My little children, let us not love in word, neither in tongue; but in deed and in truth." 1 John 3:11, 16-18

God expressed His love toward us by giving us Jesus Christ to lay down his life for us. In the same manner, we are commanded to express our love toward God and our brethren through giving. For love is not measured in words alone, but in action and sincerity; and sincerity is determined by consistency. Therefore, because of our love for God, we ought to be consistent in our giving to further the kingdom of God.

It is very important to God that many more people are saved before time runs out. Whether it is for areas of internal ministry (the growing and maturing of the church) or outreach ministry (the reaching out for lost souls and to ease the suffering of Mankind), it takes money to finance it. Who better to give that money than the people God loves and who loves Him?

"Each man should give what he has decided in his heart to give, not reluctantly or under compulsion, for God loves a cheerful giver." 2 Corinthians 9:7 (NIV)

God loves a cheerful giver because, at that moment, we are a reflection of His character. At that moment, we are like God—loving with our actions. At that moment, we are playing a part in the fulfillment of His plans. At that moment, we are showing God that we love Him by giving to benefit those that are made in His image.

"... Knowing that whatsoever good thing any man doeth, the same shall he receive of the Lord, whether he be bond or free." Ephesians 6:8

We must keep in mind that giving does not just benefit the person receiving the gift, but the giver as well. That is why God established a spiritual principle that says, *"Do unto others as you would have others do unto you."*

"Give, and it shall be given unto you; good measure, pressed down, and shaken together, and running over, shall men give into your bosom. For with the same measure that ye mete withal it shall be measured to you again." Luke 6:38

When we give to others in good measure, others will give to *us* in good measure. Let's look at Second Corinthians Chapter 9 again to see those benefits promised to us when we give to others:

"He has scattered abroad his gifts to the poor; his righteousness endures forever."Now he who supplies seed to the sower and bread for food will also supply and increase your store of seed and will enlarge the harvest of your righteousness. You will be made rich in every way so that you can be generous on every occasion, and through us your generosity will result in thanksgiving to God. This service that you perform is not only supplying the needs of God's people but is also overflowing in many expressions of thanks to God. Because of the service by which you have proved yourselves, men will praise God for the obedience that accompanies your confession of the gospel of Christ, and for your generosity in sharing with them and with everyone else. And in their prayers for you their hearts will go out to you, because of the surpassing grace God has given you. 2 Corinthians 9:6-14 (NIV)

Here Paul describes giving as sowing seeds into the lives of others that will not only supply their needs, but also inspire their faith and thanksgiving to God. In turn, God will make all grace abound toward us so that we will have everything we need. God will make us rich in every way so that we can be generous on every occasion, and the hearts of the people who received from us, will go out to us in prayer for us.

So remember this: Whoever sows sparingly will also reap sparingly, and whoever sows generously will also reap generously. Each man should give what he has decided in his heart to give, not reluctantly or under compulsion, for God loves a cheerful giver. *"And God is able to make all grace abound to us, so that in all things, at all times; having all that we need, we will abound in every good work."* 2 Corinthians 9:8

Now, if that's not an incentive to give, I don't know what is! If we sow as we purpose in our heart, we will get back much more than what we gave, and even still, there is yet a higher level of sowing.

Chapter Ten

SOW OUT OF OBEDIENCE TO THE VOICE OF GOD

———————————— ⊕ ————————————

Foundation Scripture: Leviticus 25:18-22

Wherefore ye shall do my statutes, and keep my judgments, and do them; and ye shall dwell in the land in safety. And the land shall yield her fruit, and ye shall eat your fill, and dwell therein in safety. And if ye shall say, What shall we eat the seventh year? Behold, we shall not sow, nor gather in our increase: Then I will command my blessing upon you in the sixth year, and it shall bring forth fruit for three years. And ye shall sow the eighth year, and eat yet of old fruit until the ninth year; until her fruits come in ye shall eat of the old store.

This requires us to hear God and be sensitive to the leading of the Holy Spirit. This can only come by Confessing, Meditating and observing to do what the Word of God says. God spoke to Moses:

"And the LORD spoke unto Moses in Mount Sinai, saying, "Speak unto the children of Israel, and say unto them, When ye come into the land which I give you, then shall the land keep a Sabbath unto the LORD. Six years thou shalt sow thy field, and six years thou shalt prune thy vineyard, and gather in the fruit thereof; But in

the seventh year shall be a Sabbath of rest unto the land, a Sabbath for the LORD: thou shalt neither sow thy field, nor prune thy vineyard." Leviticus 25:1-4

God wanted the land to keep a Sabbath, so He instructed the children of Israel to only sow for six years. The seventh year was the Sabbath. The Sabbath is the time when everyone is supposed to rest from their labors i.e. Sabbath Day or the land is supposed to rest from being farmed i.e. Sabbath Year.

I believe that this is how we get the "Hundredfold" return because it takes a certain level of faith to sow out of obedience to God's voice. When God instructs us to sow, the tendency is to try to figure out how the blessings will return or how we will sustain ourselves until our harvest comes in. In fact, trying to figure out how everything will go *before* we obey God is our enemy; as it causes a blockage to progress.

We are not made to be in "search mode" and "doer mode" at the same time. God's instruction requires immediate obedience and when we try to figure out how things are going to work out, we hesitate. Hesitation, no matter how brief, allows doubt to come in and wage a battle with your faith in an effort to overcome you with fear and disbelief.

Fear, doubt and disbelief are the forces that keep many people from experiencing the tremendous breakthroughs that comes from sowing out of obedience to The Voice of God. Always remember that fear, doubt and disbelief are not emotions, they are spirits that oppose you when you make an effort to progress.

Remember, when we got saved we believed and acted first, then the understanding of what we did came later as we studied the Word of God and sought the Lord through prayer. The same is true through a lifestyle of walking with God; we must believe and act immediately on the written and spoken Word of God, and then we will receive the understanding of what we did *afterwards*.

The children of Israel sowed into ground that normally produced a harvest for one year. However, when they obeyed God's voice and sowed like God instructed them to, God commanded His blessing upon their seed sown, multiplied the harvest and brought forth fruit for three years instead of one! This is a revelation: obedience to God's spoken Word will enlarge the capacity of our seed to produce exponentially.

In January 2004, my pastor appealed to the congregation to give a special offering over and above our normal tithes and offerings, so that the church could purchase new vans. The Lord spoke to me in that service to give $300. Yes, it took a lot of faith to obey His Voice because I didn't have much money at that time. (Faith obeys God immediately. Faith does not focus on self-perceived limitations.)

The timing of the pastor's request was interesting to me, because I was believing God for a larger vehicle. I had four children at the time. They were too young to ride in the front seat of the car and there was not enough room for them to ride safely in the backseat. We needed an SUV.

My pastor taught that when we sow a seed, the seed must fall to the ground and die before it starts to grow. In essence, when we sow money, we have to do without it for a while until the harvest comes. The money must become dead to us.

So when the Lord spoke to me to give the $300, it required immediate obedience, lest I rationalized myself out of it. I had no time to plan and knew that I may not even see my harvest for some time. Even though it was spontaneous, I was happy to give it because I knew that the church needed the new vans to pick up the people who didn't have cars. I wanted to do my part and help. Also, I knew that God loves a cheerful giver, so it didn't make sense to be sad and fretful over that decision.

Six months later, the Lord began pressing on my heart to make a transition into ministry. Soon I left my position as Regional Vice President at the company where I worked. I became an independent contractor with the idea of working part-time while making my transition into ministry.

In just the first forty days of being an independent financial advisor, I made over $30,000. That is a one hundredfold return on the $300 seed that I sowed out of obedience to the voice of God. I went and purchased my SUV and put down half of the purchase price before eventually paying it off totally. The church got the vans that were needed, I got my SUV, and God was glorified. Isn't that wonderful? The same way that principle worked for me, it will work for anyone who is quick to obey the voice of God.

The Bible tells us that Isaac received a hundredfold return for sowing out of obedience to the voice of God. Here's his account:

"And there was a famine in the land, beside the first famine that was in the days of Abraham. And Isaac went unto Abimelech king of the Philistines unto Gerar. And the LORD appeared unto him, and said, Go not down into Egypt; dwell in the land which I shall tell thee of: Sojourn in this land, and I will be with thee, and will bless thee; for unto thee, and unto thy seed, I will give all these countries, and I will perform the oath which I swore unto Abraham thy father;" Genesis 26:1-3

"Then Isaac sowed in that land, and received in the same year a hundredfold: and the LORD blessed him. And the man waxed great, and went forward, and grew until he became very great: Genesis 26:12-13

Isaac didn't just reap a hundredfold return for sowing; instead, he reaped it for sowing in **obedience**. His sowing was out of obedience to the voice of God to stay in that land even though there was a famine. His sowing in the mist of a famine was an act of faith. By his actions, he was saying that he believed and trusted God who told him to stay there. As a result, the Lord commanded His blessing upon Isaac's seed, and Isaac reaped a hundredfold in that same year.

It's important to note that we aren't supposed to just sit around waiting on God to speak to us—audibly or otherwise—so that we can get a hundredfold return. In fact, Jesus sheds light on this in the parable of the sower:

"And he spake many things unto them in parables, saying, Behold, a sower went forth to sow; And when he sowed, some seeds fell by the way side, and the fowls came and devoured them up: Some fell upon stony places, where they had not much earth: and forthwith they sprung up, because they had no deepness of earth: And when the sun was up, they were scorched; and because they had no root, they withered away. And some fell among thorns; and the thorns sprung up, and choked them: But other fell into good ground, and brought forth fruit, some a hundredfold, some sixtyfold, some thirtyfold." Matthew 13:3-8

"Hear ye therefore the parable of the sower. When any one heareth the word of the kingdom, and understandeth it not, then cometh the wicked one, and catcheth away that which was sown in his heart. This is he which received seed by the way side. But he that received the seed into stony places, the same is he that heareth the word, and anon with joy receiveth it; Yet hath he not root in himself, but endureth for a while: for when tribulation or persecution ariseth because of the word, by and by he is offended. He also that received seed among the thorns is he that heareth the word; and the care of this world, and the deceitfulness of riches, choke the word, and

he becometh unfruitful. But he that received seed into the good ground is he that heareth the word, and understandeth it; which also beareth fruit, and bringeth forth, some a hundredfold some sixty, some thirty." Matthew 13:18-23

No, we don't have to sit around waiting for God to speak to us because we have His Word already, and His Word is His will for us. When we confess and meditate on it, we are sowing the Word into our heart. A heart that readily receives God's Word and observes to do what it says; is what Jesus referred to as good ground.

Observing to do what it says shows that we believe and understand God's Word and fruit (results) automatically grows out of obedience…some thirtyfold, some sixtyfold and some a hundredfold.

Nowhere in the Bible does it say that in order to be successful in anything, you need a PhD, or a Master's degree from college. That's what the world wants you to believe because that is the world's system. Having a degree is certainly not a bad thing; however, it is not a biblical prerequisite for success.

Don't misunderstand me, education is a wonderful tool, and indeed there is great worth to academic learning. The problem is that the world's way is sometimes complicated. It says, "Go to school for years; spend more years getting a degree; then "hopefully" get a good job!" That "hopefully" part is a stretch because most college graduates I know seldom work in the areas in which they received their degree.

The Kingdom of God's way is simple. It says, "The Sower Soweth the Word and brings forth some thirty, some sixty, and some a hundredfold." There is great power and truth with the Word of God. That's the big difference.

I meditated on Luke 6:38:

"Give, and it shall be given unto you; good measure, pressed down, and shaken together, and running over, shall men give into your bosom. For with the same measure that ye mete withal it shall be measured to you again."

I purposed in my heart that every time the church's offering plate or bucket passed in front of me, and/or I heard the Word of God preached, I would give money. There are also other times when I can hear a dollar amount spoken in my spirit. That dollar amount, and instructions as to where I should sow it, comes across as clear as if it were spoken to me audibly by someone on the inside of me. (I refer to this as the voice of the Lord or the voice of His Word.) As a result of my willingness and obedience to give, I have increased every year and my children are prospering as well.

When we sow God's Word into our hearts, it creates new thought patterns that start speaking to us automatically. Also, the Word itself has a voice and will start speaking to us.

My pastor meditated on this scripture prior to moving his family to Chicago:

"And Jesus answered and said, Verily I say unto you, There is no man that hath left house, or brethren, or sisters, or father, or mother, or wife, or children, or lands, for my sake, and the gospel's, But he shall receive a hundredfold now in this time, houses, and brethren, and sisters, and mothers, and children, and lands, with persecutions; and in the world to come eternal life." Mark 10:29-30

It wasn't long before the Word he meditated on began instructing him to leave his job to preach the Gospel. He obeyed, left his job and moved his family to Chicago with only $200 to his name. He started a Bible class that very quickly grew into a church. That wasn't more than fifteen years ago. He is now a multimillionaire through his obedience.

The church is positioned within a once-abandoned mall, which the Lord showed my pastor step by step how to purchase. Its revived retail community pays the church. The church owns a Christian elementary school, a private jet, a bank, a production company and several other businesses. The church has grown to over 12,000 members and my pastor is continuously planting new churches. But most importantly, he owns and operates an international ministry that reaches countless millions in many countries and that also brings countless souls to Christ every year!

My pastor confessed the Word of God and meditated it. After a while, when he heard the Voice of the Lord and the Voice of His Word, he observed to obey it by sowing his job and committing his life for the sake of the gospel. He still reaps a hundredfold return as everything that pertains to him continues to increase supernaturally.

Part II - Action Points

Tithing is defined as giving ten percent of your increase (income) to the house of The Lord. Some people give it to the place or places where they receive spiritual food i.e. their local church or a television ministry. I give all of my tithes to my local church and sometimes split my offerings between my local church and other ministries.

There have been questions about whether we should tithe on the gross or net amount of our income. My answer to that is the Bible instructs us to tithe on *all* of our increase. I defined increase as any money that comes into my hand or into any account where I store money i.e. direct deposits, 401(k), health spending accounts, etc.

You shall truly tithe all the increase of your seed that the field brings forth year by year. Deuteronomy 14:22

Consistency is important when it comes to tithing. It is the only place in the Bible where the Lord instructs us to prove (test) Him.

"Bring one-tenth of your income into the storehouse so that there may be food in my house. Test me in this way," says the LORD of Armies. "See if I won't open the windows of heaven for you and flood you with blessings..." Malachi 3:10

What is also important is that we are open to change and to new opportunities. Many times, the Lord will give us ideas and opportunities that may not fit in with our existing channels of income. If we don't try to limit Him and be open to His leading, He will lead us into places where the rewards are astounding.

1. How have the teachings in Part II of this book changed the way you think of tithes and offerings?

   _____

   _____

   _____

   _____

   _____

2. After your tithes are paid, how much specifically are you committed to giving as offerings? Where will you give your offerings?

_____

_____

_____

_____

_____

3. After six months of consistency, what are your realistic expectations for increase? Is it a promotion? Is it increased revenue? A better job? Healing for you and other family members? Contracts approved, etc.?

_____

_____

_____

_____

4. On occasion, The Lord will prompt you to give to special projects at the local church and/ or other ministries. When He does this, He is creating an opportunity for multiplication in your income. However, the request is usually not a comfortable one; you will have to trust Him that you will recover exponentially. Will you be open to giving the amount He prompts you to give even if you feel that you can't afford it?

_____

_____

_____

_____

_____

Additional Notes

PART THREE

PRINCIPLE
OF SAVING

Part III

PRINCIPLE #2
THE PRINCIPLE OF SAVING

Foundation Scripture: Deuteronomy 28:8

"The LORD shall command the blessing upon thee in thy storehouses, and in all that thou settest thine hand unto; and he shall bless thee in the land which the LORD thy God giveth thee."

As a Registered Principal of an investment firm, I used to conduct financial education seminars. The statistic below is one I used in those seminars to really drive home the importance of saving:

At the current rate of wealth creation, by the year 2005, out of 100 workers at age 65:

1 — Will be wealthy (Net worth of $5 million or more)

4 — Will be financially independent (Net worth of $1 million to $4.9 million)

41 — Will be working

54 — Will be DEAD BROKE

Clearly, according to the statistic, 54% of Americans have no savings at all and another 41% didn't save properly.

Some people have never learned to save properly. They are not dead broke, but they are not financially independent either. This group of people either has very high debt compared to the income they earn, or they haven't yet learned to reign in excessive spending.

Saving money and resources is a principle. More specifically, it is one of the ways we increase. This principle is not always instinctive; rather, it is a learned behavior that takes self discipline in order to master it. There are many who learn to be good savers from their upbringing. They are taught at a young age to always save a portion of their earnings.

For example, I have a friend whose uncle owns a nightclub. His nightclub earned a reputation among its patrons as being one of the most exciting places to be. For years, people would fill his nightclub to capacity. However, as time passed, jobs began to leave the city and the nightclub's attendance waned, as did other businesses.

One day, as we were all at my friend's house for a barbeque, I asked the uncle how was it that he could afford to stay open when the nightclub's attendance was so low. He said that during the years his nightclub did well he prepared himself for times like these. He saved enough money to sustain himself for several years until his nightclub's attendance began to increase again. During those low years, he never closed down like many of the other nightclubs.

The more exposure I had to my friend's family, the more I observed that they all treated money the same way. They treated money as a valuable tool that was not to be squandered. They treated money as if it was designed to provide for their basic needs— as well as their other desires—but not to be used up in the process. They understood that without money, they would all be at the mercy of their circumstances.

A great lesson can be learned when observing people like this. They possess a key that is not as common as many may think. That key is forethought. Forethought allows us to successfully practice the Principle of Saving. The Bible happens to have plenty to say about forethought.

"Go to the ant, thou sluggard; consider her ways, and be wise: which having no guide, overseer, or ruler, provides her meat in the summer, and gathers her food in the harvest." Proverbs 6:6-8. The ant provides for her meat in the summer and stores up her food in the harvest time. She is diligent to provide and diligent to save a portion of everything she brings in. She has forethought.

Another scripture says, *"The Lord shall command the blessing upon us in our storehouses..."* Deuteronomy 28:8 What is a storehouse? In today's language, it would be a savings account or another type of investment vehicle. It could also be a place where we accumulate resources and other provisions.

Nowhere does the Bible tell us to *get* a storehouse. It automatically assumes that we have one, which means that *every* person should have one. Or better yet, we should have several, because the scripture says, *"the Lord will command the blessing on your storehouses."* Note it is plural.

In the book of Proverbs, storehouses are referred to as barns. *"Honor the LORD with your substance, and with the firstfruits of all your increase: So shall your barns be filled with plenty, and your presses shall burst out with new wine."* Proverbs 3:9-10

We must have barns in order for God to fill them. They become full, not based on how much money we *earn*, but based on how much we *keep*. It doesn't matter how much God increases our income if we don't have a safety net to catch some of it. Savings and investment accounts, storehouses and barns—they are our safety nets.

In addition to saving *our* money, we must teach our children to save *their* money as well. If we don't teach them to save, they will more than likely squander the inheritance we leave them.

"A good man leaves an inheritance to his children's children..." Proverbs 13:22. We have to save in order to leave an inheritance to our children's children. But the purpose of our savings is not limited to investment opportunities and amassing large amounts of money for our families.

No, one of the main reasons we save is to fund the Gospel and other charities that seek to ease the suffering of Mankind. How will we be able to fund the gospel if we don't change our financial stability through saving money?

Jesus' ministry required people to fund it. Chapter Eight in the Book of Luke states that there were many people who gave to Jesus out of their substance. Those people couldn't have given if they had not first saved. Remember, the tithe was paid to the temple. So what they gave Jesus had to be their offerings from their discretionary income and their savings.

Chapter Eleven

YOUR MONEY MUST BE ASSIGNED

---⊕---

Foundation Scripture Proverbs 27:23

"Be diligent to know the state of your flocks and look well to your herds."

After servicing over a thousand clients in the Financial Services industry, it became clear to me that those who were successful savers understood that money must be assigned. Unless our money is assigned, we will not be successful savers and the spirit of poverty will affect our lives.

Poverty has nothing to do with how much money we earn. It has everything to do with our mental bondage. It is a negative stronghold. It is a negative thought pattern.

People who have a "poverty mentality" **think** that they should spend every dime they earn. This is called the "consumption mentality."

I have seen people who make $140,000 per year have the same financial stress as a person who makes $16,000 per year. We would be surprised to know how many people, with strong cash flows, were only one or two paychecks away from being homeless.

Whenever people with a consumption mentality envision themselves in relation to money they never see themselves as being frugal with their clothes-buying or being generous with their savings. They don't envision themselves investing the money and then tracking its growth, either. On the contrary, they seem to always see themselves spending lots of money without a care in the world; buying up their heart's desires and giving money freely to friends and family.

Financial freedom begins with changing the way we think about money and how we assign it – or use it. Of course, money must be consumed. We all need food, shelter, clothing and other necessities to help us navigate safely down the river of life. However, at the same time, we must check ourselves against conspicuous consumption and the impulsive release of our financial seed into the world. We must live below our means.

Some money must be sowed if we are to have financial increase. Some must be saved if we are to have financial stability. Without financial stability, we can find ourselves at the mercy of our circumstances; never able to give toward the spreading of the gospel.

The principles of stewardship are parallel. It doesn't matter whether we apply it to money or time. For instance, if we don't have a plan or an assignment for our time before our day begins chances are we are going to waste some or all of it. It's the same with money. If we don't have a plan or an assignment for our money before we get it then chances are we will waste some or all of it. In fact, people who waste time usually waste money.

"He also that is slothful in his work is brother to him that is a great waster." Proverbs 18:9

Again, in order to manage money successfully it must be assigned. Following is a sheet I use when assigning my money, as it helps me to have forethought. It should be completed and referred to the day before you are paid wages.

First, observe your **obligations**. Your obligations are (in this order): tithes, savings, debts such as your mortgage or rent, car note, credit cards etc.

Next, observe your **living expenses**. Your living expenses are: grocery, heating, electricity, phone, gas, and insurance bills.

Create a budget with the intention of plugging up all the holes and filling in all the gaps that your money seems to fall through every month.

Example: If your net income is $3,000 per month and your debt is $1,688 per month, then:

Take 10% of the $3,000, which is $300, and pay tithes. That leaves $2,700. Take another 10% of the $3,000, which is $300, and pay yourself by saving the money. That leaves $2,400. Paying your debt of $1,688 leaves $712. Your living expenses total $500, which leaves $212. (This is what I call the 10/10/80 Rule. The first 10% is the Tithe, the second 10% is for saving, and then you live off of the remaining 80%. This is the easiest rule to follow for anyone wishing to bring order to their finances.)

With the remaining money that is left over (surplus), give an offering, save it, have some entertainment or whatever you desire--with godly intentions of course.

Notice that I didn't refer to your initial savings as surplus. Your savings is your primary obligation after you pay tithes. Your offerings should only be given out of your surplus unless God leads you to give from your savings, or until you have saved more than enough to cover three to six months worth of living expenses. (If you are married, you and your spouse should be in agreement about withdrawing from your savings.)

1. Living Expenses

Housing
Rent $
Telephone
Utilities
Maintenance & Repair
Furnishings
Improvements
House hold help
Other

Total home-related expenses $

Family
Food & grocery $
Clothing
Medical & dental expenses
(not covered by insurance)
Laundry & dry cleaning
Child care
Education expenses
Legal Expenses
Other (alimony, child support, etc.)

Transportation
Gas & oil $
Maintenance & Repair
Other (travel, auto, etc.)

Giving
Tithes $
Charitable
Non-charitable

Leisure
Vacations $
Hobbies (club memberships, etc.)

Entertainment
(restaurants, cable, movies, etc.)

Other
Total non-home-related expenses $

2. Debt Payments   *Now*

Mortgage
Other debt payments
    B. Total debt payments $

3. Insurance Premiums

Individual life $
Group life

Auto & homeowners
Other (disability, health, etc.)
    C. Total insurance premiums $

4. Savings

Emergency fund $
Retirement $
College
Other goals & dreams
    D. Total savings $

5. Taxes

Income $
Property
Other
    E. Total taxes $

6. Income

Primary $
Spouse
Other
    G. Total income $

7. Short Fall or Surplus

A. Total living expenses	$
B. Total debt payment	$
C. Total insurance premiums	$
D. Total savings	$
E. Total taxes	$
F. Total expenses (A+B+C+D+E)	$
G. Total Income	$

(Stay tuned for Time Management in Chapter Twenty.)

Chapter Twelve

MIRROR WHAT YOU GIVE

⊕

Foundation Scripture: Matthew 19:19

"... and, Thou shalt love thy neighbour as thyself."

We shall love our neighbor as we love ourselves. If we love our fellow man enough to give him money to help ease his suffering, we should love ourselves enough to save our money to prevent our own suffering. We should at the very least do for ourselves what we do for others.

The best way to start a great savings program is to mirror what you give. The 10/10/80 Rule is a perfect way to start. The 10/10/80 Rule says that whatever you are paid or receive as income you distribute those funds as follows:

The first 10% to your church or local ministry (this is the tithe)

The second 10% to your savings plan

The other 80% to meet your living obligations

I began to take mirroring a step further and applied it to every giving contribution I made. When I gave my 10% in tithes, I saved the same amount. When I contributed to the offerings, I saved the same amount. When I gave to the poor on the street or to needy families, or even to my own family members, I would make a similar contribution to my own savings. I even mirrored my many gifts to my children. Every time I paid them their allowance, I would pay myself by saving the same amount.

It worked so well that before I realized it, I had quite a bit of money saved! If you would try it, you would be surprised at how much accumulates in such a short period of time. Now, how do you make your savings work for you?

I always recommend using the three-category approach when beginning to save money.

Short-Term   Mid-Term   Long-Term

1. Now – maintain a basic savings account which can provide liquid emergency funds.

2. Short-Term – is used for personal items like clothing, holiday gifts, birthday presents, special occasions, and special projects like purchasing a car or house. Money Market accounts and Short-Term Bond Funds are perfect for this category.

3. Long-Term – These funds are designed to accumulate over time. They include accounts like an IRA (Individual Retirement Account), College Savings Plans, 401k, Mutual Funds, Stocks, Annuities and Universal Life Insurance policies.

Our savings is where we measure our financial progress. It doesn't matter how much money we make, but rather how much we keep. If we don't contribute to our savings systematically, then we are no further ahead today than we were yesterday.

We must discipline ourselves! This will not work without discipline, especially if saving is something you are not accustomed to doing systematically.

I understand that there are many people who only save if there is something left over after they have met their obligations.

I am not recommending that you start off mirroring at a higher level and applying it to every monetary gift as I have done. I am, however, suggesting that you mirror based on your own level of tithing first and then as you grow accustomed to that, increase your savings to mirror your giving in other areas in addition to the tithe. Will it mean living with less money for those impulse buys? Maybe, or maybe not.

When people envision prosperity, most of them think of large sums of money appearing all of a sudden while others think of high income streams flowing into their lives. That is a description of success. That is not a description of prosperity. Prosperity comes before success! Prosperity is the growth that brings us up from where we are to the level of success God intended for us.

Success does not show up for most people because they have yet to engage the principles of prosperity. For others who we consider fortunate enough to have success show up without practicing prosperity, are not able to hold on to it very long. The ones who are able to hold on to their success are the ones who make the mental adjustment and transform themselves from consumers to investors.

If we think that our income has to be substantially higher before we become disciplined savers, we should reconsider. We will one day look back at all of the money we failed to keep and realize that we have missed prosperity. To begin saving money and living below our means is to begin prosperity. For it is a choice that we can CHOOSE TO BEGIN NOW!

Most of us have dreams of financial independence. What is your dream? I have found that having a dream, a vision, or a clear mental picture of what we desire to achieve works as a strong incentive to be a disciplined saver. Impulsive spending does not stand a chance when we have a big vision and a solid plan of action that we feel an emotional connection to.

Chapter Thirteen

THE JOSEPH PRINCIPLE

---⊕---

Foundation Scripture: Genesis 41:34

"Let Pharaoh do this, and let him appoint officers over the land, to collect one-fifth of the produce of the land of Egypt in the seven plentiful years."

The Joseph Principle is found in Genesis chapters 41 through 47. I will refer to quite a few verses as I share with you the benefits of this principle.

While Joseph was imprisoned in Egypt, Pharaoh (The King) had two recurring dreams. Dreams were assumed to be messages from God so Pharaoh relied heavily on his priests or magicians to interpret them. When they couldn't do so, Joseph was given the chance, since his gift of interpreting dreams had been demonstrated before the prison guards.

"Then Pharaoh sent and called Joseph, and they brought him hastily out of the dungeon: and he shaved himself, and changed his raiment, and came in unto Pharaoh. And Pharaoh said unto Joseph, I have dreamed a dream, and there is none that can interpret it: and I have heard say of thee, that thou canst understand a dream to interpret it. And Joseph answered Pharaoh, saying, it is not in me: God shall give Pharaoh an answer of peace." Genesis 41:14-16

When Pharaoh commended Joseph on his reputation that preceded him, Joseph humbled himself. He made it clear that the interpretation of Pharaoh's dream and the solution to its riddle came from God.

"And Joseph said unto Pharaoh, The dream of Pharaoh is one: God hath showed Pharaoh what he is about to do. The seven good kine are seven years; and the seven good ears are seven years: the dream is one. And the seven thin and ill favored kine that came up after them are seven years; and the seven empty ears blasted with the east wind shall be seven years of famine. This is the thing which I have spoken unto Pharaoh: What God is about to do he showeth unto Pharaoh. Behold, there come seven years of great plenty throughout all the land of Egypt: And there shall arise after them seven years of famine; and all the plenty shall be forgotten in the land of Egypt; and the famine shall consume the land; And the plenty shall not be known in the land by reason of that famine following; for it shall be very grievous. And for that the dream was doubled unto Pharaoh twice; it is because the thing is established by God, and God will shortly bring it to pass. Now therefore let Pharaoh look out a man discreet and wise, and set him over the land of Egypt. Let Pharaoh do this, and let him appoint officers over the land, and take up the fifth part of the land of Egypt in the seven plenteous years." Genesis 41:25-34

As Joseph explained the mystery of Pharaoh's dreams, he was inspired by God to instruct Pharaoh to save the "fifth part." The fifth part is equal to 20% in the plenteous years. The act of saving the fifth part—twenty percent of your income—is what I refer to as "The Joseph Principle."

What is so significant about the fifth part? Well, first and foremost, five is the number of Grace. In other words, it represents the grace of God. This is very significant as evidenced by several pivotal references in scripture. Let's review five of those references:

1. David chose five smooth stones to use with his sling to knock off Goliath. Those stones represented the grace of God being present with him to kill Goliath, who was much larger and stronger than him. The slaying of that giant Philistine allowed Israel to defeat the Philistine army and it also promoted David.

    "And he took his staff in his hand, and chose him five smooth stones out of the brook, and put them in a shepherd's bag which he had, even in a scrip; and his sling was in his hand: and he drew near to the Philistine." 1 Samuel 17:40

2. *The Holy Anointing Oil was pure and composed of five parts whose measurements were in multiples of five. Whoever the oil was poured upon, the Grace and Anointing of God would rest upon him.*

   "Moreover the LORD spoke unto Moses, saying, Take thou also unto thee principal spices, of <u>pure myrrh</u> five hundred shekels, and of <u>sweet cinnamon</u> half so much, even two hundred and fifty shekels, and of <u>sweet calamus</u> two hundred and fifty shekels, And of <u>cassia</u> five hundred shekels, after the shekel of the sanctuary, and of <u>oil olive</u> a hin (five quarts): And thou shalt make it an oil of holy ointment, an ointment compound after the art of the apothecary: it shall be a holy anointing oil." Exodus 30:22-25

3. Five represents God's Grace during this dispensation of Grace where the gentiles can be saved. There are five ministry gifts given for the perfecting of the saints, for the work of the ministry and for nurturing—as in building up to equip or edify—the body of Christ.

   "And he gave some, (1) <u>Apostles</u>; and some, (2) <u>Prophets</u>; and some, (3) <u>Evangelists</u>; and some, (4) <u>Pastors</u> and (5) <u>Teachers</u>; for the perfecting of the saints, for the work of the ministry, for the edifying of the body of Christ." Ephesians 4:11-12

4. There were five offerings that represented God's Grace to cover up the sins of Israel and to cause them to appear as a holy people unto God.

   Five Offerings = (1) Burnt Offering *(Leviticus 1:4-9)*, (2) Meat (Meal) Offering *(Leviticus 2:1-16)*, (3) Peace Offering(*Leviticus 3:1-17)*, (4) Sin Offering *(Leviticus 4:1-4)*, and (5) Trespass Offering *(Leviticus 6:1-7)*.

5. In case you're still trying to understand the significance of five as the number of Grace, God spelled it out for us by inspiring Paul to write the word "Grace" five times in Romans Chapter 11, starting at verse five. It's more than coincidental because "Grace" is not mentioned before or after these verses in this chapter.

   Here God, through Paul, is pointing out to us clearly that it is because of Grace that you are blessed with things that you cannot work for.

   "Even so then at this present time also there is a remnant according to the election of (1) grace. And if by (2) grace, then is it no more of works: otherwise (3) grace is no more (4) grace. But if it be of works, then is it no more (5) grace: otherwise work is no more work." Romans 11:5-6

It is important to understand how saving the fifth part accomplished so much. It is evident that God's grace is on the fifth part.

Joseph instructed Pharaoh to save the fifth part of everything during those seven years of plenty. When Pharaoh complied, the first thing that happened as a result of "The Joseph Principle" was that his savings multiplied.

"And Joseph gathered corn as the sand of the sea, very much, <u>until he left numbering; for it was without number.</u>" Genesis 41:49

Joseph kept track of what was saved. He left numbering, not because he was careless, but because there were no known numbers in their language to count that high.

The second thing that happened as a result of "The Joseph Principle" is that Joseph had provisions for his family: His father Jacob (Israel), stepmothers, his brothers, his wife, his children, his nephews and nieces, for 300 years. All who pertained to his family had provisions for generations, even though they grew in number from sixty six people that came with Jacob during the famine, to over a million by the time that they were put into slavery just before Moses was born. They had provisions and lacked nothing.

The third thing that happened as a result of "The Joseph Principle" is that Joseph was able to save lives and help many people on an international scale.

"And all countries came into Egypt to Joseph for to buy corn; because that the famine was so sore in all lands." Genesis 41:57

The fourth thing that happened as a result of "The Joseph Principle" is that Joseph was in position to negotiate and multiply the assets under his charge.

"And Joseph gathered up all the money that was found in the land of Egypt, and in the land of Canaan, for the corn which they bought: and Joseph brought the money into Pharaoh's house. And when money failed in the land of Egypt, and in the land of Canaan, all the Egyptians came unto Joseph, and said, Give us bread: for why should we die in thy presence? for the money faileth. And Joseph said, Give your cattle; and I will give you for your cattle, if money fail. And they brought their cattle unto Joseph: and Joseph gave them bread in exchange for horses, and for the flocks, and for the cattle of the herds, and for the asses: and he fed them with bread for all their cattle for that year. When that year was ended, they came unto him the second

year, and said unto him, We will not hide it from my lord, how that our money is spent; my lord also hath our herds of cattle; there is not aught left in the sight of my lord, but our bodies, and our lands: Wherefore shall we die before thine eyes, both we and our land? buy us and our land for bread, and we and our land will be servants unto Pharaoh: and give us seed, that we may live, and not die, that the land be not desolate. And Joseph bought all the land of Egypt for Pharaoh; for the Egyptians sold every man his field, because the famine prevailed over them: so the land became Pharaoh's. And as for the people, he removed them to cities from one end of the borders of Egypt even to the other end thereof. Only the land of the priests bought he not; for the priests had a portion assigned them of Pharaoh, and did eat their portion which Pharaoh gave them: wherefore they sold not their lands." Genesis 47:14-22

The fifth thing that happened as a result of "The Joseph Principle" is that Joseph was able to make laws for the land.

"Then Joseph said unto the people, Behold, I have bought you this day and your land for Pharaoh: lo, here is seed for you, and ye shall sow the land. And it shall come to pass in the increase that ye shall give the fifth part unto Pharaoh, and four parts shall be your own, for seed of the field, and for your food, and for them of your households, and for food for your little ones. And they said, Thou hast saved our lives: let us find grace in the sight of my lord, and we will be Pharaoh's servants. And Joseph made it a law over the land of Egypt unto this day, that Pharaoh should have the fifth part; except the land of the priests only, which became not Pharaoh's." Genesis 47:23-26

In Egypt, the law of the fifth part being taxed is still in existence today. Individuals and corporations alike are taxed at twenty percent.[2]

Joseph was able to make laws in a land that wasn't even his own. We, as Christians, have got to understand the significance of this! If we desire change to occur with the laws in our land, let us enlist a few holy billionaires and holy trillionaires to get the job done. With that kind of money and manifestation of godly wisdom, all we have to do is speak the word. With that type of power, we could enact a law to ban pornography from the Internet! Every school would have prayer once again! Every courtroom would post the Ten Commandments without question! We could ensure that a whole new FCC team cleans up all the perverted television and radio programming! We could make laws that would affect society for the better!

All of this is possible if we would simply begin by saving the fifth part of our income. I pray that God will enable you to see what I see. I encourage you to ask Him, as I have, for a clear mental picture of what can be accomplished with this principle. We must see it with our mind and in our heart first before we can seize it in our life.

Part III - Action Points

Assigning our money is the first step toward successful saving. Saving money takes commitment and the rewards are tremendous.

1. Write down your savings goals for the next twelve months (should be a minimum of 10% of your income) then get started right away with saving in each category every time you receive income.

   $ _____ short-term

   $ _____ mid-term

   $ _____ long-term

2. Create a spreadsheet. Down the left side of the spreadsheet make a small column to place dates in them. In the next column, each time you give money somewhere (offerings, charitable donations, gifts to extended family, children, loans to friends, etc.) log the destination. In the third column, log the dollar amount given. In the fourth column, list which area of savings (short-term, midterm or long-term) you have deposited that same amount of money (remember, your savings should mirror your giving.)

   _____ Put a check mark here when your spreadsheet has been created.

3. Set up short-term, mid-term, and long-term savings accounts with different financial institutions. (Never put all of your eggs in one basket. If one bank fails or experiences computer system issues, more than likely it will not affect the other accounts and you would still have access to cash if you need it.)

   _____ Put a check mark here when your accounts have been set up.

4. Once you have accomplished consistency with mirroring your giving, engage the Joseph Principle by saving a minimum 20% of your income. (At this stage, you will want to implement a number of financial planning instruments and strategies to get the maximum rate of return on your

savings. I will discuss a number of those strategies in the *Make Your Way Prosperous Workbook.*)

Just a word of advice – try not to touch your savings. Establish separate short-term accounts for holidays, birthdays, clothing, car maintenance, etc. Make a habit of paying expenses from income and short-term accounts only. Do not use emergency funds, mid-term, and/or long-term savings for anything other than what they are designated for.

_____ Put a check mark here when this has been accomplished.

Additional Notes

PART FOUR

PRINCIPLE OF AGREEMENT

PRINCIPLE #3
THE PRINCIPLE OF
AGREEMENT

Foundation Scripture Psalm 133:1-3

"Behold, how good and how pleasant it is for brethren to dwell together in unity! It is like the precious ointment upon the head that ran down upon the beard even Aaron's beard: that went down to the skirts of his garments; As the dew of Hermon, and as the dew that descended upon the mountains of Zion: for there the LORD commanded the blessing, even life forevermore."

Unity is good and pleasant.

When the Bible calls something good, it is not referring to "good" as we know it. We have various degrees of good, i.e. good, great, greater, and greatest. The Bible refers to "good" as that which is pleasing to God; in harmony with His Word; and beneficial to all men. There is no middle ground with God--either it is completely good, or it is completely evil.

Unity is good because it reflects God.

God manifests Himself as "God-The Father" for the sake of creation; "God-The (Word) Son" for the sake of salvation; and "God-The Holy Spirit" for the sake of regeneration. Although His manifestations have three distinct functions, His manifestations are united for the cause of reaping the souls of men.

It is clearly stated in 1 Corinthians 15:28 that, when all things are finally subdued, resumption will take place. In that instance, as the kingdom is being delivered up to God, He will no longer have three manifestations with three distinct functions. Instead, He will be all in all.

And when all things shall be subdued unto him, then shall the Son also Himself be subject unto him that put all things under him, that God may be all in all. 1Corinthians 15:28

Unity is pleasant because it is an expression of harmony.

In other words, to be in unity means there is agreement and harmony between people. It is crucial to understand how to obtain and maintain unity. We obtain unity by eliminating strife and adopting a "like-precious faith." We maintain unity by operating in agreement with each other in accordance to God's Word.

Chapter Fourteen

ELIMINATE STRIFE

---⊕---

Foundation Scripture Galatians 5:19-21

"Now the works of the flesh are manifest, which are these; adultery, fornication, uncleanness, lasciviousness, Idolatry, witchcraft, hatred, variance, emulations, wrath, <u>strife,</u> seditions, heresies, Envyings, murders, drunkenness, revellings, and such like: of the which I tell you before, as I have also told you in time past, that <u>they which do such things shall not inherit the kingdom of God.</u>"

This is a powerful scripture because one would think that this speaks to a later judgment that is going to take place in the future. That is one of the reasons why so many have lost the fear and reverence of the Lord, because judgment for their behavior is not immediate. Also, the enemy is very skilled at deceiving people into thinking that they have time and that they can put off repentance until some later date. However, this passage of scripture doesn't refer to judgment, but rather to loss.

When we receive salvation through Jesus Christ of Nazareth, we receive an inheritance. That inheritance is not exclusively reserved for us in some distant future, but is something that we can walk in right now.

Our inheritance is eternal life which supersedes time. Eternal life is superior to time in that it exists before time began, exists during time and exists after time ends. We have begun living our inheritance of eternal life already, although we also live in this realm of time. Our inheritance is our covenant of peace, which means prosperity, health, safety, happiness, favor, wellness, and rest. It is our covenant of wholeness, which means nothing missing, nothing broken, and nothing lacking.

When believers walk in strife, they cannot walk in their inheritance. Strife is not a part of our inheritance nor is it permitted in our covenant of eternal life. So when you observe someone walking in strife, you will notice things in their life that are missing, broken and lacking. Why? Because our dual citizenship allows us to walk in the benefits of eternal life right here on Earth and dwell in the Kingdom of God simultaneously. Since strife is earthly and devilish, it stands opposed to our Kingdom benefits and by default blocks our blessings.

God gave us His Word to follow, not because He wants to steal our fun, but because He knows that sin is injurious to us. So He created a scenario; whereas, we can have a place reserved for us in heaven while we enjoy some of heaven's benefits here on Earth. Being in this scenario constitutes our immediate gain. To *not* be in that scenario—where we can take advantage of all those benefits—is an immediate loss.

That's what Galatians Chapter 5 Verse 19 through 21 is talking about. It points out that people, who practice the works of the flesh, cause themselves to suffer an immediate loss. Their strife causes a break in their hedge. A "hedge" is a spiritual fence that surrounds us to protect us.

He that diggeth a pit shall fall into it; and whoso breaketh a hedge, a serpent shall bite him. Ecclesiastes 10:8

The key point to realize is that we are the ones who break our own hedge. Somehow, we know that to be true in our spirit because when we feel the enemy biting in areas where he shouldn't be, our first reaction is self-examination.

One of the things I have observed to be a pattern with married people is that when there is strife in the home, the first thing that the enemy attacks is the family's finances. Secondly, their children are the target. Thirdly, the couple's covenant with each other gets challenged and unfortunately, at times, distorted.

Let's take a look at what the scriptures say about strife. The Word tells us that strife causes rebellion and strife also causes leadership to suffer.

For ye rebelled against my commandment in the desert of Zin, in the strife of the congregation, to sanctify me at the water before their eyes: that is the water of Meribah in Kadesh in the wilderness of Zin. Numbers 27:14

They angered him also at the waters of strife, so that it went ill with Moses for their sakes: Psalm 106:32

Strife is burdensome and drains your mental, physical and emotional energy.

How can I myself alone bear your encumbrance, and your burden, and your strife? Deuteronomy 1:12

Strife has a mushroom effect. When strife is released, the effect of it grows and grows.

The beginning of strife is as when one letteth out water: therefore leave off contention, before it be meddled with. Proverbs 17:14

Strife causes confusion, which then allows every evil work to creep in.

For where envying and strife is, there is confusion and every evil work. James 3:16

For God is not the author of confusion, but of peace, as in all churches of the saints. 1Corinthians 14:33

Sowing strife is the same as sowing discord, for strife causes discord.

These six things doth the LORD hate: yea, seven are an abomination unto him: A proud look, a lying tongue, and hands that shed innocent blood. A heart that deviseth wicked imaginations, feet that be swift in running to mischief, A false witness that speaketh lies, and he that soweth discord among brethren. Proverbs 6:16-19

Why does the Lord have such extreme hatred for strife and discord? It goes further than the fact that the end result is physical, mental, emotional harm and devastation to those involved. When Lucifer sinned, God changed his name to Satan and put him out of heaven. The name Satan is defined as "one who sows discord.

So when a person causes strife by sowing discord, not only does their act resemble Satan; but just like Lucifer harmed himself and suffered loss when he did it, so does the person harm themselves and suffer loss. God would love for us to choose to avoid this path altogether, rather than seeing us harm ourselves. That's why He hates it so much.

Strife resides in the heart.

But if ye have bitter envying and strife in your hearts, glory not, and lie not against the truth. James 3:14

Strife is when adversity or opposition is acted out either intellectually or physically in order to gain superiority over others. Whether it's in the home, church, neighborhood or job, it doesn't matter. The person causing the strife is trying to gain superiority over another. What's interesting is that sometimes the person causing this kind of strife is not even aware that competitive jealousy and envy is what is motivating their behavior.

Competitive jealousy is when a person feels like someone else is surpassing them in some area. The competition could be socially, intellectually, economically or physically driven. It could be something as vain as physical appearance. But whatever it is, such a person feels inferior and causes strife to slow the other down, stop what the other is doing, cause others to dislike the other person, or any other means of gaining superiority.

Envy works in a similar fashion. People who are envious simply want what others have. They don't want to do the work to get their own. Both envy and strife have their root in pride.

He that is of a proud heart stirreth up strife: but he that putteth his trust in the LORD shall be made fat. Proverbs 28:25

Pride is like bad breath in that we're usually the last person to know we have it. But like bad breath, pride can be remedied. All one would need to do to rid themselves of pride is to follow a few simple steps:

1. First, we must confess our sin to God as soon as we discover that there is pride in our heart.

If we confess our sins, he is faithful and just to forgive us our sins, and to cleanse us from all unrighteousness. 1John 1:9

2. Secondly, we must wash our heart by the continual confession and meditation of scriptures on humility and love.

That he might sanctify and cleanse it with the washing of water by the word. Ephesians 5:26

3. Thirdly, we must shut our mouths.

   "Where no wood is, there the fire goeth out: so where there is no talebearer, the strife ceaseth." Proverbs 26:20

   "If you think you are being religious, but can't control your tongue, you are fooling yourself, and everything you do is useless." James 1:26 CEV (Contemporary English Version)

4. Fourthly, we must keep our mind on Jesus.

   Thou wilt keep him in perfect peace, whose mind is stayed on thee: because he trusteth in thee. Isaiah 26:3

   When a person takes their mind off of people and puts their mind on the Lord, the Lord will keep them in perfect peace. Why is that so important? It is important because if a person has peace in their heart, then they will speak peace.

   "A good man out of the good treasure of his heart brings forth the good. And an evil man out of the evil treasure of his heart brings forth the evil. For out of the abundance of the heart his mouth speaks." Luke 6:45 MKJV

5. Last but certainly not least, we must act out love and humility by valuing others with the proper respect and friendship.

   "Let nothing be done through strife or vainglory; but in lowliness of mind let each esteem other better than themselves." Philippians 2:3

Chapter Fifteen

LIKE-PRECIOUS FAITH

---- ⊕ ----

Foundation Scripture 2 Peter 1:1

"Simon Peter, a servant and an apostle of Jesus Christ, to them that have obtained like precious faith with us through the righteousness of God and our Savior Jesus Christ:"

Like-precious faith is a powerful concept. It is when two or more believers have the same level of faith. It is something that must be obtained; however, we won't do so by desire alone. It's a divine allotment that comes upon a believer based on the word of faith that we are taught, the word of faith that we meditate, and the word of faith that we practice or walk in daily.

That is why we will only find like-precious faith among those who are under the same teaching, the same study regimen and/or the same prayer habit. By "same teaching" I don't mean the same pastor or teacher, but the same message, which is the message of "the righteousness of God by faith."

But now the righteousness of God without the law is manifested, being witnessed by the law and the prophets; Even the righteousness of God which is by faith of Jesus Christ unto all and upon all them that believe: for there is no difference: Romans 3:21-22

99

As believers, the sooner we realize that one of the purposes of the Word of God is to change what we believe in our heart, the easier life will be for us and we will mature at a faster pace.

God knows that we will only go as far in life as we believe we can. As long as we are walking in our purpose, there are no limits to how far we can go once we get the revelation of "the righteousness of God by faith."

When Adam sinned in the beginning, we all sinned in him. How? Every seed produces after its own kind. An apple produces apples, oranges produce oranges, wheat produces wheat, apes produce apes, not people (which make the theory of evolution invalid) and people produce people. Even green grapes produce green grapes, not purple ones. The same truth applies to Mankind. Sinful Mankind produces sinful Mankind, not righteous Mankind.

So when the Bible says in Romans 3:23, *"For all have sinned, and come short of the glory of God;"* it is not an issue regarding the acts we committed, but rather an issue of how we were born into this world. That is why Jesus said in John 3:7 *"Marvel not that I said unto thee, Ye must be born again."*

Why must we be born again? We must be born again because God really loves us and He wants us to be with Him. He didn't create Hell for *us*; He created Hell for the devil and the devil's angels.

Then shall he say also unto them on the left hand, Depart from me, ye cursed, into everlasting fire, prepared for the devil and his angels: Matthew 25:41

God created Earth for us; He also created a place in Heaven for us; and He wants us to dwell together with Him. However, there is one problem: God is righteous and sinful man cannot survive in the presence of The Holy and Righteous God. So, to dwell together with Him, He had to make us righteous.

God knows that a problem can't be solved on the same level that it was created. In order to solve any problem, it has to be dealt with on a level above that which it was created. Just like money answers all things in the world's system, faith and love answers all things in the Kingdom of God's system.

For in Jesus Christ neither circumcision availeth any thing, nor uncircumcision; but faith which worketh by love. Galatians 5:6

The Law of Faith supersedes the Law of Sin and Death. You can take the Law of Faith and use it to break free from the Law of Sin and Death.

For the law of the Spirit of life in Christ Jesus hath made me free from the law of sin and death. Romans 8:2

God expressed His love toward us by making the biggest sacrifice. He gave His beloved Son, Jesus Christ, to die for sin in our place so that we may live through Him.

In this was manifested the love of God toward us, because that God sent his only begotten Son into the world, that we might live through him. Herein is love, not that we loved God, but that he loved us, and sent his Son to be the propitiation (atoning sacrifice) for our sins. 1 John 4:9-10

So when we confess with our mouth that Jesus Christ is Lord and believe in our heart that God raised Him from the dead, we become born again. In other words, we are saved; redeemed from our sinful nature and given a righteous one.

"That if thou shalt confess with thy mouth the Lord Jesus, and shalt believe in thine heart that God hath raised him from the dead, thou shalt be saved. For with the heart man believeth unto righteousness; and with the mouth confession is made unto salvation." Romans 10:9-10

When we became born again, Jesus Christ took our sins and declared us righteous. This happens strictly through faith.

"Being justified freely by his grace through the redemption that is in Christ Jesus: Whom God hath set forth to be a propitiation through faith in his blood, to declare his righteousness for the remission of sins that are past, through the forbearance of God; To declare, I say, at this time his righteousness: that he might be just, and the justifier of him which believeth in Jesus." Romans 3:24-26

That is why we must be born again. It makes us righteous so that we can stand in the presence of God through Jesus Christ. This is important because a revelation of the righteousness of God through faith in Jesus Christ is necessary for faith to operate.

"Jesus answered and said unto him, Verily, verily, I say unto thee, <u>except a man be born again, he cannot see the kingdom of God.</u>" John 3:3

In order to obtain our allotment of like-precious faith, we have to know that we are entitled to that which we seek. That can't be done through sin consciousness, because sin consciousness brings condemnation and condemnation separates us from fellowship with God.

Sin consciousness produces guilt, and guilt produces condemnation. When we condemn ourselves, we cease to receive the gift of righteousness that is freely given to us who believe. This breaks our fellowship with God. Faith cannot survive in your heart without fellowship with God.

Just like sin was not an issue of our acts, but an issue of how we were born, so is the case with righteousness. It is not an issue of acts, because we can never obtain righteousness by our own works. We receive righteousness when we become born again through faith.

Now that we understand this, let's tie it into our inheritance. The righteousness of God through Christ Jesus gives us entitlement to our inheritance.

"The Spirit itself beareth witness with our spirit, that we are the children of God: And if children, then heirs; heirs of God, and joint-heirs with Christ; if so be that we suffer with him, that we may be also glorified together." Romans 8:16-17

"Joint-heir" does not mean that we all get a portion of the inheritance. Joint-heir means that we co-own it all. With Jesus Christ we co-own all things!

"Therefore let no man glory in men. For all things are yours; Whether Paul, or Apollos, or Cephas, or the world, or life, or death, or things present, or things to come; all are yours; And ye are Christ's; and Christ is God's." 1 Corinthians 3:21-23

That means healing is mine. Peace is mine. Joy, prosperity, safety, rest, wholeness, is all mine because it is part of my inheritance.

Jesus said that we should know the truth and the truth shall make us free. The truth that we know shall make us free. James commands us not to lie against the truth. The Word of God is truth.

"But if ye have bitter envying and strife in your hearts, glory not, and lie not against the truth." James 3:14

"Sanctify them through thy truth: thy word is truth." John 17:17

When we are of like-precious faith, we know that the righteousness of God through Christ Jesus entitles us to all things. We don't speak what we see and lie against the truth; we speak the truth by speaking the Word, even if we can't see the manifestation of it yet.

We should never say, "I am sick," because it is a lie against the truth. The truth says, "I am healed!" The truth says, "I am strong!" The truth says, "I am rich!" The truth says, "I am holy!" The truth says, "I shall not lack any good thing!"

We want people of like-precious faith to agree with us in prayer. We don't want to pray in agreement for ten thousand dollars by Thursday with someone who can only believe God for one hundred dollars by Saturday.

When we are of like-precious faith, we don't see a difference in what we ask, because all things are ours. It is imperative that we grasp hold of this precept!

Here's an example in simpler terms. If I took your car without permission and drove it to my house, what would you do? You would come get your car without hesitation, right? Why? Because you are entitled to it; it belongs to you. So what is the difference between your car that you are entitled to and the promises in the Word of God that you are entitled to?

There is no difference. God's promises in His Word are just as real to you as your car. Just like you have to come take your car back from my house, you have to go and take the promises of God by faith. The righteousness of God through Christ Jesus *is* our entitlement.

When we are of like-precious faith, we realize that there is no difference in that faith. We are eager to agree with one another because we know that if just two of us shall touch and agree on anything, God will bring it to pass.

Again I say unto you, That if two of you shall agree on earth as touching any thing that they shall ask, it shall be done for them of my Father which is in heaven. Matthew 18:19

Chapter Sixteen

ONE ACCORD—PART I

---⊕---

Foundation Scripture: Genesis 11:1-5

"And the whole earth was of one language, and of one speech. And it came to pass, as they journeyed from the east, that they found a plain in the land of Shinar; and they dwelt there. And they said one to another, Go to, let us make brick, and burn them thoroughly. And they had brick for stone, and slime had they for mortar. And they said, Go to, let us build us a city and a tower, whose top may reach unto heaven; and let us make us a name, lest we be scattered abroad upon the face of the whole earth. And the LORD came down to see the city and the tower, which the children of men built."

Language is the gateway. If you want access to anything—whether it is a computer, a career, a culture, a principle, etc.—you must first learn the language of it and the doors will be opened unto you.

Whenever students learn a new subject at school, they are first presented with the terms used with the subject and the definitions of those terms. Why? Again, as I just mentioned, the language of a thing gives one access to understanding. In order to operate or excel in a thing you must first understand how it works.

The first verse of Genesis Chapter 11 says that the whole earth was of one language and one speech. This is profound in and of itself because when the Bible refers to the whole earth in this context, it's referring to the people and not the land. (It's written the same way in Revelation 6:8 where the word earth is referring to the people and not the land.)

So, all the people of the earth were of one language and one speech. One language means all the people spoke the *same* language. However, when talking about "one speech," that carries a deeper meaning.

Romans 10:17 says that faith comes by hearing the Word of God. I believe that those seventy scholars who translated the King James version back in the 1600's, translated the verse more accurately when they said, "faith cometh by hearing, and hearing by the Word of God.

Faith comes by hearing. What is faith? Faith is "belief that produces a corresponding action." "Belief that produces a corresponding action" comes by hearing. Hearing what? Hearing words.

But the "God kind of faith" comes by hearing the Word of God, because God's Word is truth. The continual hearing of God's Word produces a self-image that is holy, a belief without limits, and actions that are righteous.

It doesn't matter what words we hear, if we continuously hear them, they will produce belief in us, accompanied by a corresponding action. In life, we will only go as far as we believe we can. Also in life, we'll only believe what we continuously hear.

Someone once said (believing they were giving good advice), "be careful of what you believe." That, I must say, was not the best advice. The best advice is for us to first and foremost take heed of what we *hear*—as Luke 8:18 (KJV) warns us—because what we hear (and continue hearing) will then determine what we believe.

The fact that they had one language to listen to in Genesis Chapter 11 was a key to their accord because they could understand each other's speech or each other's motives. So the more they spoke, the more they heard. The more they heard, the more they believed. The more they believed, the more their value system produced an image on the inside that was consistent with their belief.

Therefore, their belief system caused them to act and speak based on the image on the inside. That is why Paul said in 2 Corinthians 4:13 (KJV), *"we believe therefore we speak."* That is why Jesus said in Luke 6:45 (KJV), *"out of the abundance of the heart, the mouth speaks."* That is why David said in Psalm 140:1-2 (KJV), *"the evil and violent man who is continually gathered together for war, does so out of the* imagination or **image** of mischief **in their heart."**

Our speech and our actions are a reflection of the image we have in our heart. That is why it was written this way: "the whole earth was of one language and one speech." Not because they were all robots and did everything the same, but because they all had the same image and therefore had the same speech (motives). They all spoke the same thing regarding a particular matter, a particular concern, or a particular cause in which they acted upon.

The next thing that is important to observe is that they were a "collective body," which means they were community-minded. They were many, who were united as one. There was no "I" or "Me" in their speech.

"And they said one to another, Go to, let us make brick, and burn them thoroughly. And they had brick for stone, and slime had they for mortar. And they said, Go to, let us build us a city and a tower, whose top may reach unto heaven; and let us make us a name, lest we be scattered abroad upon the face of the whole earth." Genesis 11:3-4

Working together successfully towards a particular cause requires one speech. On the other hand, self-centeredness opens the door to division. In order to eliminate division from the collective body, everyone must be totally giving of themselves for the sake of the cause and totally submitted to one leader—such as Nimrod in Genesis 10:8-10— who was sold out to the cause.

"One language" made it easy for them to encourage one another. "One speech" means that they did it repetitively for the sake of the cause.

Faith (belief accompanied by a corresponding action) is not stored in our hearts. It is a force like strength. Just as we must continually eat in order to produce and replenish strength to our physical bodies, we must continually hear words or speech, in order for our hearts to produce and replenish faith for our spiritual being.

Those people in Genesis Chapter 11 collectively spoke as one, which encouraged everyone to continue to excel as one. As they acted immediately on what they heard as one, there was such a force that it triggered a reaction from Almighty God.

"And the <u>LORD came down</u> to see the city and the tower, which the children of men built." Genesis 11:5

It doesn't say that "The Lord *looked down* from heaven," it says that "The Lord *came down.*" Imagine what that means for us in regards to all the good causes in our society that need our support. When a group of individuals get on one accord and begin to operate in a collective manner, it gets God's attention!

Another example is Acts 2:1, where the Apostles were all gathered in the upper room and on one accord. The Holy Spirit fell upon them and they began to speak with unknown tongues and do exploits.

Last but not least, I have to mention Peter and John in Acts Chapter 4. After healing an impotent man, they were arrested and put into holding overnight. After being threatened, they were released and went to their own people and told them everything that happened to them. When their people heard this, they all lifted up their voice to God and prayed on one accord. After praying, the whole place was shaken; they were filled with the Holy Ghost and preached the Word of God with boldness. There was great grace given unto them and they had no lack.

This is a spiritual key in that we can receive supernatural power and help to get things done with speed, if we could get on one accord with one another.

Chapter Seventeen

ONE ACCORD—PART II

---⊕---

Foundation Scripture: Genesis 11:6-7

"And the LORD said, Behold, the people is one, and they have all one language; and this they begin to do: and now nothing will be restrained from them, which they have imagined to do. Go to, let us go down, and there confound their language, that they may not understand one another's speech."

Verses 6 and 7 of Genesis Chapter 11 are so powerful and full of revelation, but I would venture to say most people just read them at face value. Follow along, as I have dissected these verses so we can look at them one section at a time; one revelation at a time.

"And the LORD said,"

If God says something, He is talking from His point of view. This means that the statement He is about to make is truth. This is important because He is acknowledging a principle and the effects of it.

"Behold, the people is one,"

109

God created language. So why did He say, "the people **is** one," instead of saying, "the people **are** one?" In order to answer that, let me back up to the beginning of existence to lay a clearer foundation.

When God created ADAM, He created ADAM after the likeness—the very being—of God. That means whatever God could do, so could ADAM do here on earth. God also gave ADAM **dominion** over all the earth.

"Dominion over all the earth" means dominion over everything inside the circumference of the earth. It means dominion over animals, birds, fish, insects, water, weather, time, air, nature, land, minerals, metals, money, resources, trees, plants, etc.

When ADAM sinned, he lost his *supernatural* power and could only operate in *earthly* power, which means that he lost his dominion over time, space, nature, water, weather—everything. When Christ, "The Second ADAM" came, all power in Heaven and Earth was given to Christ so that through Him dominion over time, space, nature, water and weather could be restored to us. He also acquired for us dominion over death, hell, the devil and the devil's works.

That supernatural power from Heaven allowed Jesus to walk on water and not sink; speak to a tree and that tree wither; speak to a storm and that storm cease; turn water into wine; heal the sick; cast out demons; and so much more. When Jesus went to the cross for us, that dominion granted to Him was transferred to us.

Now, I believe that there are two types of power that flow through dominion. There is an **earthly power** that flows as a result of exercising the principle of agreement in the likeness of the image of ADAM (self-image), and there is a **supernatural power** that flows as a result of exercising the principle of agreement in the likeness of God through the image of Jesus Christ.

This supernatural power happens only when believers come together in unity and on one accord.

"ADAM" represents "The God-like force" or "The God-like spirit in Man." "Jesus Christ (The Second ADAM)" represents "The Son of God," which is "God Himself." In essence, The First ADAM is <u>like</u> God. The Second ADAM <u>is</u> God.

So when we do things out of self-image, we become one with ADAM and operate as a God-like force in earthly power. When we are in covenant with God through salvation in Jesus Christ, we do things out of the image of Christ. In other words, we become one with The Second ADAM and operate as God in supernatural power.

That's why God said, "the people is one." When He saw the people operating in unity out of self-image, He saw them as ADAM. He saw them as a God-like force operating in earthly power.

"and they have all one language;"

They are united in the things that they speak. They understand one another and they share the same cause.

"and this they begin to do:"

This shows how powerful the principle of One Accord is. So powerful that, in spite of everything those people had accomplished in building that tower, God said that they were just beginning. When you operate on One Accord, there is no limit to how far and how fast you can go. Their efforts seemed to be accelerated.

"and now nothing will be restrained from them,"

Nothing means "no thing" or "not one thing." Not one thing will be restrained from them.

Keep in mind when God said, "and now nothing will be restrained from them," He was saying, "not one thing will be held back from them. I can't withhold anything from them, and neither can the devil, because they are operating on One Accord, they are operating in unity, they are operating in agreement in the place where they were given dominion.."

All this time, we thought we were waiting on God, but in essence, God has been waiting on us to get on One Accord. He knows that when the Church gets on One Accord, great exploits will take place! Wealth will flow like never before. Healing will flow like never before. Power will flow like never before. Love will flow like never before. Not one thing will be held back from us; not even a wholesome society.

"which they have imagined to do."

This phrase speaks to the thoughts and ideas that were produced by the people's image. Their image didn't produce random or scattered thoughts and ideas; it produced thoughts that were in alignment with their cause.

It seemed like everything was wonderful and in order, since being on one accord was a good thing, right? With that being the case, what was it about their imagination that God didn't like? The problem was their imagination was birthed out of self-image, which was rebellious and full of pride.

Let's look at Genesis 9:1 and Genesis 10:8-10 for more insight.

"And God blessed Noah and his sons, and said unto them, Be fruitful, and multiply, and replenish the earth." Genesis 9:1

"And Cush begot Nimrod: he began to be a mighty one in the earth. He was a mighty hunter before the LORD: wherefore it is said, Even as Nimrod the mighty hunter before the LORD. And the beginning of his kingdom was Babel," Genesis 10:8-10

The name "Nimrod" means, "Let us rebel." The word "mighty" means powerful by implication; warrior or tyrant. The word "hunter" means to lie alongside in wait, as if to catch an animal. Figuratively, though, it means to catch and murder men.

Thus the phrase, *"Even as Nimrod the mighty hunter before the Lord"* can be properly translated, *"Even as Nimrod the mighty hunter opposed to the Lord."* Not only was Nimrod rebellious, but he led his people in rebellion against the Lord, as well.

Now, when the people came together in agreement, they wanted to stay together in one city. Thus, their rebellion began. That's why there was a rush to build a tower. They chose to make it with brick, which was faster than quarrying stones. They hurried "lest we be scattered." That implied that they knew the will of the Lord (Genesis 9:1) for them to multiply and replenish the earth.

They wanted to build a city, which would be their center of unity. They wanted to make their own name great, which revealed their arrogance, pride, and ego. Finally, they wanted to build a tower to reach heaven out of defiance, as if to say that they can get there without God. (When we observe the world's intentions today, it doesn't seem like much has changed!)

They had an evil imagination that was born out of an ungodly self-image. Unfortunately though, because they were in agreement and on "one accord," the Lord had already declared that nothing would be restrained from them.

Let's now get back to the remaining phrases of verses 6 and 7 of Genesis Chapter 11...

"Go to,"

"Go to," means to "come now." The phrase should read, "Come now, let us go down..."

"let us go down,"

Here is a powerful revelation regarding this principle. Remember that God was talking, right? Who was God talking to when He said, *"let us go down?"* He was talking to Himself. God self-talks.

Why did He call Himself "us"? God was revealing that He is a collective— the Trinity.

"For there are three that bear record in heaven, the Father, the Word, and the Holy Ghost: and these three are one." 1 John 5:7

Now there are some who would ask, "How is it that three are one?" I would reply, "the same way that we are three in one: spirit, body and soul."

God is The Father, the Word, and the Holy Ghost. We are unified tripod beings who were created in the image of Him. Each part of our being has a distinct function, so does His. We are one person, so is He. We have one personality, so does He. *"Just as He is, so are we in this world."* 1 John 4:17

When death occurs, our spirit and soul are separated from our body. Our body ceases to exist, but our spirit and soul live on. God can never die. It is also impossible for God to be separated. He is all-powerful; always present everywhere, all knowing, and all wise. That is why whenever He does anything, establishes anything, or creates anything; it is always completed in the best way that it could possibly be done.

God constructed the components of salvation in the manner of trilogy: spirit, water and blood. He knows that the most powerful principle in the earth is the principle of agreement. Those three elements in agreement make salvation everlasting.

"And there are three that bear witness in earth, the spirit, and the water, and the blood: and these three agree in one." 1John 5:8 (KJV)

This is the reason Christianity can't be stopped; God put all the components of salvation into agreement. That's why it is necessary for one to get Water Baptized and Spirit Filled, because those components are in agreement with the Blood of Christ that cleanses us from all sin.

"and there confound their language, that they may not understand one another's speech."

Any time God deals with change, He deals with it at the root. Their language was their only gateway to agreement, but the real root of the problem for those people was their image. The word that they spoke (their speech) is what produced their faith (belief with a corresponding action) in their cause. Their words also constructed their image.

God had to mix their language so that they wouldn't understand one another's speech. He knew that if they couldn't understand what they heard, their faith in what they were doing would cease; their image would change; and the prideful actions that corresponded with their cause would stop as well.

Is it God's desire that we be divided? No! God wants us to be unified… as long as our intentions are good.

"Now I beseech you, brethren, by the name of our Lord Jesus Christ, that ye all speak the same thing, and that there be no divisions among you; but that ye be perfectly joined together in the same mind and in the same judgment." 1Corinthians 1:10

Chapter Eighteen

ONE ACCORD—PART III

---⊕---

Foundation Scripture: Genesis 11:8-9

"So the LORD scattered them abroad from thence upon the face of all the earth: and they left off to build the city. Therefore is the name of it called Babel; because the LORD did there confound the language of all the earth: and from thence did the LORD scatter them abroad upon the face of all the earth."

How do we speak the same thing being different people, from different nationalities, from different walks of life, at various levels of maturity in our Christian journey? We speak the same thing by not speaking our own opinion. We speak the same thing by not speaking what we see, but instead by speaking faith. We speak the same thing by speaking the Word of God.

When we speak according to the Word of God, the Word will create in us a new image in which to act upon. It will cause us to join together in love. As long as we speak the Word <u>and obey the Word</u>, we will have the same mind and the same judgment. Obedience is an important part of this equation, because disobedience perverts judgment.

The only compliment that the Bible gives Satan's kingdom is that it's not divided against itself. For instance, you'll never hear about a demon casting out another demon!

"And He called them unto Him, and said unto them in parables, How can Satan cast out Satan? And if a kingdom be divided against itself, that kingdom cannot stand. And if a house be divided against itself, that house cannot stand. And if Satan rise up against himself, and be divided, he cannot stand, but hath an end." Mark 3:23-26

Now watch this. *"For he said unto him, Come out of the man, thou unclean spirit."* Mark 5:8

Jesus called demons an unclean spirit (singular) not unclean spirits (plural). He did so because He saw them as one.

"And he asked him, What is thy name? And he answered, saying, My name is Legion: for we are many." Mark 5:9

It doesn't say <u>they</u> answered (plural); it says <u>he</u> answered (singular). They didn't say, "<u>Our</u> name is Legion (plural)," <u>he</u> said, "<u>My</u> name is Legion (singular)." Legion (3,000-5,000 demons) means that they were regimented and unified and marching in ranks for the same cause. They all spoke and acted as one.

At times, we may think we're fighting one little demon that strayed off course, but according to Mark 3:23-27 and Mark 5:9 that's not likely the case. Instead, the host of Hell may have been marching against us and it sounded like one enemy, but it was many. That's why Jesus said that we must first bind The Strong Man.

"And if a house be divided against itself, that house cannot stand. And if Satan rise up against himself, and be divided, he cannot stand, but hath an end. No man can enter into a strong man's house, and spoil his goods, except he will first <u>bind the strong man</u>; and then he will spoil his house." Mark 3:25-27

The "Strong Man" is the term Jesus used for the one (demon) who holds the authority or leadership over certain demons. So if we bind the "Strong Man" over a negative situation or condition, we, by default, bind every demon under the Strong Man's authority.

We are fully equipped to bind the strong man. As 1John 4:4 reminds us, we have a higher power. *"Ye are of God, little children, and have overcome them: because <u>greater is He that is in you, than he that is in the world."</u>*

Even with our higher power, we sometimes tire in our struggle. Whenever that happens, we just need to remember that according to Matthew 18:19, we don't have to struggle.

"Again I say unto you, That if two of you shall agree on earth as touching any thing that they shall ask, it shall be done for them of my Father which is in heaven."

"One can chase a thousand and two can chase ten thousand." (Deuteronomy 32:30)

If one of us can chase a thousand demons and two of us can chase ten thousand demons, imagine what would happen if *all* of us got together in Agreement! Just think how many drug demons we would chase; how many poverty demons we would chase; how many strife demons we would chase; how many sickness demons we would chase; and on and on.

In your devotional time, read the story of Sodom and Gomorrah in Genesis Chapter 19. It gives us an example of The Principle of Agreement used negatively. The people were all in agreement in their perverse self-image. Their language was "us" and "we." They were all on one accord, both old men and young men alike. In doing so, it triggered the judgment of fire and brimstone from on high.

Next, read the story of the day of Pentecost in Acts Chapters 1 and 2. It gives us an example of The Principle of Agreement used positively. One hundred and twenty people were gathered together and on one accord in the image and cause of Jesus Christ. In doing so, it triggered the infilling of the Holy Ghost and an outpouring of miracles.

Negative agreement triggered judgment. Christ-like agreement triggered the promise from on high and other miracles. I hope by now you've got a firm grasp of that. However, I would be remiss if I didn't explain how The Principle of Agreement is a shortcut.

Remember in the Old Testament (Exodus Chapters 25-28) how there was an establishment of The Most Holy Place and the High Priest? Well, there was a certain etiquette that had to be followed there. All the families had to bring an offering to God and the High Priest was the only one who could go into The Most Holy Place into the presence of God.

It's written that King David discovered a shortcut into the presence of God. Instead of going through all of the ceremonies here's what he did:

"Enter into his gates with thanksgiving, and into his courts with praise: be thankful unto him, and bless his name." Psalm 100:4

David could get into the presence of God with thanksgiving and with praise. He didn't have to wait for a ceremony of offerings. He could praise God in song, gladness or in worship at any time.

Thanksgiving and Praise was the shortcut in the Old Testament and it is a shortcut in the New Testament. However, The Principle of Agreement is the greatest shortcut in the New Testament.

The Principle of Agreement is simple. We don't have to go through five steps to a financial turn around, seven steps to debt freedom, ten steps to a blessed marriage, twelve steps to healing and fifteen steps to bring in the wealth of the wicked. We don't have to do all of that. All we need to do is connect with other believers and agree, and our Heavenly Father shall do it. Period.

"Again I say unto you, That if two of you shall agree on earth as touching any thing that they shall ask, it shall be done for them of my Father which is in heaven." Matthew 18:19

"Behold, how good and how pleasant it is for brethren to dwell together in unity! It is like the precious ointment upon the head, that ran down upon the beard, even Aaron's beard: that went down to the skirts of his garments; As the dew of Hermon, and as the dew that descended upon the mountains of Zion: for there the LORD commanded the blessing, even life forevermore." Psalm 133:1-3

It doesn't say that The Lord *will* command the blessing, even life forevermore. It says that The Lord commanded the blessing, even life forevermore. The word "commanded" is written in past tense. That means it was an action that was completed in the past and cannot be undone in this present time or in the future. The latter half of that phrase, *"Even life forevermore,"* can be accurately translated as saying: *"even multiplied results will perpetually occur, as long as you are in agreement."*

There are many people in situations where they are wishing that God would move on their behalf. They are waiting and waiting on God, when in actuality

God is waiting on them. He has already commanded the blessing to happen for us upon the point of agreement. Now, all we have to do is find a like-minded Christian to agree with us on our desired outcome and God will bring it to pass.

Part IV - Action Points

Unity is powerful and it begins with eliminating strife. I got rid of the strife in my life and my income jumped 500% in ten months. I also realized my thoughts were clearer than they had been in years. I could see clearly the steps I needed to take and how to go about taking them.

Many people are struggling emotionally and financially not knowing that the answer to their prayers is a simple choice away. Eliminate the strife.

1. What has changed in your thinking as a result of understanding the principle of unity? Write three things you will change now as a result of this teaching.

_____

_____

_____

_____

_____

2. Now that we know that strife may be the culprit for delayed financial increase, what is the cause of strife in your life? What are your options for getting rid of it?

_____

_____

_____

_____

3. Find scriptures that help you walk in love, kindness and patience toward others. Confess, meditate and observe to do those scriptures. This is important because sometimes we are the source of strife in our household, so if there is going to be a change it has to begin within us. (Ephesians 4:29-32 is one of the passages I used. *"Let no corrupt communication proceed out of your mouth, but that which is good to the use of edifying, that it may minister grace unto the hearers. And grieve not the Holy Spirit of God, whereby ye are sealed unto the day of redemption. Let all bitterness, and wrath, and anger, and clamour, and evil speaking, be put away from you, with all malice: And be ye kind one to another, tenderhearted, forgiving one another, even as God for Christ's sake hath forgiven you."*)

    _____

    _____

    _____

    _____

    _____

4. Who can you find that has the same level of faith as you to agree with you in prayer? Once you find that person and they are willing to pray with you, pray for specific breakthroughs in your finances and business dealings. *"Again I say unto you, that if two of you shall agree on earth as touching anything that they shall ask, it shall be done for them of my Father which is in heaven."* Matthew 18:19 (Keep in mind; you can do this for anything you believe God for. The Bible doesn't limit this practice to finances.)

    _____

    _____

    _____

    _____

5. Define your objectives for your household and workplace in as simple terms as you can make it. (This could be a mission statement or a desired goal.)

Talk with your family to come to an agreement about what the family, as a unit, will pursue. Write down reasons and benefits for pursuing the cause. Also write down the part each family member has to play in achieving the objectives. Make sure everyone has a copy and recites it daily. Make sure everyone knows that strife is the one thing that gives the devil an opening to steal all that you've worked so hard for.

_____

_____

_____

_____

_____

You will begin to see changes take place in each person's attitude and excitement level. You will see a concerted effort to end all strife. You will also see acceleration toward your written goals. Everyone will be in agreement.

Each successful business has one thing at its core: a cause-oriented leader. If you can vocalize a cause that everyone can believe in, everyone can achieve together and everyone can benefit from that achievement, then you've got yourself a sure way toward multiplying your efforts. All it takes is a cause-oriented leader willing to lay down strife and criticism for the sake of the cause. This type of leader should inspire others through encouragement and personal example.

If they would write their own company language of "I can do all things," and incite their staff to speak the same things so that there be no division among them; that company will do exploits and nothing that they desire to do would be withheld from them.

Additional Notes

PART FIVE

DO THINGS
DIFFERENTLY

Part V

DO THINGS DIFFERENTLY

---------------------------- ⊕ ----------------------------

Foundation Scripture: Romans 12:1-2

"I beseech you therefore, brethren, by the mercies of God, that ye present your bodies a living sacrifice, holy, acceptable unto God, which is your reasonable service. And be not conformed to this world: but be ye transformed by the renewing of your mind, that ye may prove what is that good, and acceptable, and perfect, will of God."

Wealth is an offspring of thought. Covenant wealth is precious to Christians, but many fail to see it and acquire it because of their lack of covenant-thinking. People do what makes sense to them. Sometimes it never occurs to them that in order to break out of their "cycle of deficiency," they may have to do what does *not* make sense to them.

You already know by now that we, as human beings, are incapable of originating thought. We are receivers and receive thoughts from God through our spirit; from the enemy through our senses; and from our image on the inside of us.

It is easier to understand this by comparing our thought-life to computers. The reason why there is a need for computer programmers is because without a program for the computer to operate with, a command would be needed for every step that the computer would make. We take it for granted that we can just turn our computers on and type this or that. We have no idea that there are programs operating; giving hundreds of commands to the computer just so that it will function properly and complete the task that we requested.

Most of us believe what we see. We are hardwired to respond to images: designs in fashion ads; photos in political campaign ads; illustrations in books; self images on the inside; and more. What God does is create in us a new image; an image through our spirit with His Word.

Our behavior is controlled or modified by these images as they enter into our domain. How do we know which likeness we are reflecting? We know because our life is a reflection of our image just as if we were looking into a mirror.

That's how a poor person can come into instant riches through inheritance or prize winnings and so forth, and then be poor again in a couple of years. It is because their image is poverty stricken.

Try watching what happens when you take a person who has a habit of not keeping their house clean and put them into a clean new house. Soon the clean house becomes dirty and messy. Why? It is because there is no orderly standard in their image.

I recently watched a segment on Oprah where a 53-year old homeless man, who lived on the streets for over twenty years, was given one hundred thousand dollars. He could do whatever he wanted with the money. After renting an apartment, buying some clothes, buying a thirty four thousand dollar truck, visiting his family and giving money away, he was broke and homeless again after only a few months.

Oprah asked him why he hadn't spent the money with more forethought to the future. He replied that he didn't really think about that then. It did not occur to him that he would eventually run out of money. He could have invested it to grow or used it to generate income for himself.

There are people who fall into trouble and move to another city in an attempt to start over. Soon they find themselves in the same type of trouble again. Why does this happen? It's because their image needs to be renewed. What we see happening to them on the outside is a reflection of what's going on with their inner spirit.

So when the Bible talks about renewing our mind, it's talking about renewing our image. How do we do that? We renew our image through the formula for success. This formula tells us to first confess God's Word, then meditate on it day and night and then observe to do what it says. It's just that simple!

As we visualize our wealth and success, we must continue to reflect on its purposes beyond our personal comforts. Wealth is for a reason and that reason is to establish the Kingdom of God on the earth. His Kingdom is established by His Word reigning in the hearts of men, which comes from the preaching of the Gospel.

It takes an enormous amount of money to support the preaching of the Gospel and to make disciples worldwide. Remember the 10/10/80 rule? The 10/10/80 rule is where we tithe 10% of our income, save 10% and live off the other 80%. As we achieve wealth through our income stream(s) and those savings grow into assets that generate another income stream, we will share an increased 10% with those ministries we have supported. All of this is for the spreading of the gospel.

That is why we must not think it is ungodly to be rich. We shouldn't think there is anything wrong with desiring the increase that automatically comes from seeking the Lord and being obedient to His Word. Money is not evil; it is the *love* of money that is the root of all evil and the lack of money that is part of the curse.

We are supposed to love God and love one another. This is what all of the laws are written for. But how can we say that we love one another as God loves us, if we are not willing to increase so that we can be a help to our neighbors on this earth? Prosperity is our birthright. It *is* okay to buy nice things and have a comfortable life. However, we must remember that prosperity is also for a reason—God's reason, which is to harvest the souls of men.

Let's face it; people don't want to serve our God if we're broke and living in lack. Just knowing the word "broke" means penniless, ruined and out of order ought to tell us that it can't be anything associated with God, right?

For example, consider a washing machine. That washing machine is designed to wash clothes. If it stops doing what it is designed to do, we say it's broke and we call someone to fix it.

We, as human beings, were designed to have dominion in this earth. There is no dominion occurring where there is no money. If we do not have any money, or if we do not have enough money to sustain our lives as well as be a blessing to our neighbor on this earth, then we are broke. We are not being what we were designed to be and we need the Word of God to fix us.

Now this next statement that I am about to make will cause some people to laugh and some people to cry. Some of you will shake your head laughing because you can't believe it is this simple. Some of you will hang your head crying because you can't believe that you've been missing something so simple all of this time! Are you ready? Okay here it goes:

Most people don't live in abundance because they don't **plan** to. Period. They may wish it from time to time and even dream about it often, but they never sit down, write out a plan, and do it.

Chapter Nineteen

WRITE THE VISION

---------------------------- ⊕ ----------------------------

Foundation Scripture: Habakkuk 2:1-4

"I will stand upon my watch, and set me upon the tower, and will watch to see what he will say unto me, and what I shall answer when I am reproved. And the LORD answered me, and said, Write the vision, and make it plain upon tables, that he may run that readeth it. For the vision is yet for an appointed time, but at the end it shall speak, and not lie: though it tarry, wait for it; because it will surely come, it will not tarry. Behold, his soul which is lifted up is not upright in him: but the just shall live by his faith."

I have always looked at that first verse of Habakkuk Chapter 2 as a call to prayer and fasting. It's the only way that I know to effectively seek The Lord for direction and to be spiritually sensitive enough to hear Him when He speaks.

Prayer and fasting will increase our force of faith, which is what we need to receive from God. It humbles us and aids the Word in removing obstructions from our heart so that the power and goodness of God can flow through us.

All patterns of behavior (good and bad) are appetite based. This makes prayer and fasting such a purifier because if we can deny our self that which is natural (as in food), it makes it easier for us to deny our self that which is sinful.

"I will stand upon my watch, and set me upon the tower, and will watch to see what he will say unto me." Habakkuk 2:1

When I was in the Army, I had to perform "watch duty." The soldier whose shift was just before mine would wake me up at 2:00am. I would then load my weapon, go to the watch point, and scan the area for two hours. I was responsible for the lives of a whole platoon, so I would watch diligently for any movement, any sound, any change, anything out of the ordinary and so forth.

During that time, I wasn't allowed to eat anything because eating could be distracting. I had to be diligent, focused and watchful. Expecting the enemy to appear at any moment, I had to be ready at all times to stop the threat. Well, Verse One is the same concept except we're not watching for an enemy; we're watching and waiting for God.

I will pray and fast (stand upon my watch), I will praise and worship to get myself in an elevated position to hear God (set me upon the tower), and will wait and be still and watch diligently for His Words, to see what He will say unto me.

The Lord will answer, as Verse Two of Habakkuk Chapter 2 says He'll do. As surely as you are reading this book, the Lord will speak to you and give you direction.

"Write the vision, and make it plain upon tables, that he may run that readeth it." Habakkuk 2:2

For a moment, close your eyes and envision your goals or dreams. Write down the image that you see in your mind. Write down a description for that image. It is usually—but not limited to—a revelatory picture in your mind that serves as a preview of a coming attraction. It is very important you make the description of that picture as plain as you can. Posting it where it can be seen and easily read by everyone who helps to contribute to the manifestation of your vision.

Did you know that thoughts are spirit? Visions, mental pictures and imaginations are all spirit. So when you write them, you are releasing them in the earth as a seed that has the potential to grow into a harvest.

The movie "Star Trek" reveals an important spiritual concept. When the captain and his team wanted to go to a planet, they went to the transporter room. In the transporter room, someone stood at a machine and pulled up a picture of the exact coordinates of where the team was to be transported. The team, who happened to be standing on circled spaces, was then beamed (transported) to the coordinates on the picture. How did the transporter transport them? The transporter causes their bodies to dematerialize into spirit, project their spirits to the exact coordinates and then causes their bodies to materialize at those coordinates.

The spirit realm works the exact same way. In the spirit, everything travels at the speed of thought. When you visualize something, you project it in your spirit—in the spirit realm, it just happened.

Jesus said this:

"Ye have heard that it was said by them of old time, Thou shalt not commit adultery:

But I say unto you, That whosoever looketh on a woman to lust after her hath committed adultery with her already in his heart." Matthew 5:27-28.

He said this because he knew that at the moment you visualize it, it takes place in the spirit realm in your heart. That is why the writer of proverbs said this:

"For as he thinketh in his heart, so is he:" Proverbs 23:7

God inspired that statement to be written—as 2 Timothy 3:16 assures us *all* scripture is inspired of Him. He was revealing to us how it all works starting with an image.

We don't think in words, we think in pictures. We merely use words to describe the pictures we see in our minds. But we don't just think with our mind, we also think in our heart.

"And GOD saw that the wickedness of man was great in the earth, and that every imagination of the thoughts of his heart was only evil continually." Genesis 6:5

"O LORD God of Abraham, Isaac, and of Israel, our fathers, keep this forever in the imagination of the thoughts of the heart of thy people, and prepare their heart unto thee." 1 Chronicles 29:18

When we visualize something and meditate it, we lock in to the coordinates of the picture that we see and transport our spirit—at the speed of thought—to what we see. In the spirit realm, it happens instantly. The only challenge is that the physical or natural realm does not move at the speed of thought. It's much slower. That's why the vision that we see must be written. That is also why we need faith.

The writing of the vision helps us to recollect the picture we saw. Faith is needed because in the physical realm (being subject to the law of time), the manifestation of what has already taken place in the spirit realm is delayed.

In the spirit, there is no time or distance. So, the moment we think we're somewhere, we're there for a moment. The moment we envision we're debt free, we're debt free for a moment. The moment we see our self answering our calling, we're walking in it for a moment. The moment we see our self purchasing that house, we've purchased that house for a moment. The moment we see our self a millionaire, we're a millionaire for a moment.

The physical manifestation doesn't move at the speed of thought like the spirit realm. It's much slower because it is subject to time. That's why we need faith. Faith is to believe so strongly in our vision that we start acting as if it is already so; and it will be after a while. Our faith filled actions will cause us to prosper from where we are to the place we desire to be.

Faith is never blind. Faith is acting on a word that was spoken; a word that was written; or a vision that was seen. Faith is belief and action based on advance information. We don't have to know *how* it's going to happen, just believe that it *will* happen according to the word that was spoken, the word that was written, or the vision that was seen. When we start acting as if it is already so, it will be.

Not long ago, a minister spoke at my church and gave the analogy of a motorcycle act in a circus. He said that if the riders were to tell us that they were going to ride their motorcycles upside down and sideways on the inside ceiling and walls of a huge, metal ball, we wouldn't believe them.

So what did these riders do? They simply demonstrated that which we would have thought impossible if we had not seen it with our own eyes. Those riders believed what they said, and from the start, opened those bikes up in full throttle as if their task was already done, and it was so. They couldn't have gone about it half-heartedly and gotten the same results.

That is how we have to be with the visions and promises of God. Step on the gas and go full throttle as if it is already so, and it will be.

"For the vision is yet for an appointed time, but at the end it shall speak, and not lie: though it tarry, wait for it; because it will surely come, it will not tarry." Habakkuk 2:3

The vision looks for an appointment in time to manifest. When the time has come, it shall manifest exactly the way you saw it and wrote it down. Though it is a little delayed, actively wait for it by going about as if were already manifested, because it will surely manifest. It will not procrastinate beyond its time, or be later than it should, or be delayed beyond its appointment.

"Behold, his soul which is lifted up is not upright in him: but the just shall live by his faith." Habakkuk 2:4

Here is a timely warning. Did you know that the devil is already defeated? Did you know that he does not have the power to abort anything from coming to pass in our lives? He knows it. He knows that nothing can stop us, *except* us. That is why all of his wiles are designed to get us to be self-centered by honoring ourselves and our situations above honoring God and His Word.

The devil doesn't try to get mankind to become devil worshippers; he tries to get mankind to worship and praise themselves. He tries to get mankind to commit the same sin of self-centeredness and pride that caused *him* to fall.

"How art thou fallen from heaven, O Lucifer, son of the morning! how art thou cut down to the ground, which didst weaken the nations! For thou hast said in thine heart, I will ascend into heaven, I will exalt my throne above the stars of God: I will sit also upon the mount of the congregation, in the sides of the north: I will ascend above the heights of the clouds; I will be like the most High. Yet thou shalt be brought down to hell, to the sides of the pit." Isaiah 14:12

When we allow ourselves to be lifted up in pride, we dethrone God in our lives and it causes us to make a downward spiral. As believers, we don't go to hell because of our actions; however, we do become abased because we cannot prosper in pride. Visible prosperity is merely a reflection of what exists on the inside. When we fast and pray, God starts pouring into us. But when we get lifted up in pride, we cause what He poured into us to spill out.

In the scriptures, wine represents the anointing of God. With this in mind, picture your soul as a large wine glass. It has the big part that you pour your drink into, and it has the small stem that it stands on. When we fast and pray, God pours goodness and blessing and power into us.

"Behold, his soul which is lifted up is not upright in him:" Habakkuk 2:4

When we get lifted up in pride, our soul (wine glass) is no longer upright in us. It is now upside down in us, and everything God poured in, spills out. So now, God has to stop pouring and place the wine glass (our soul) right side up, so that He can start pouring again. This can take days, weeks, months, even years depending upon how quickly the individual repents.

That is why, when we see people in the same place they were last year and the year before that (spiritually, emotionally and financially), we can always find some form of pride and self-centeredness at the root of it all. The really sad part, though, is that the people in this predicament usually don't know why they haven't progressed.

Always remember that at the end of "self" is the beginning of God. The sooner we realize that, the more progress we will make. God's will for our lives is always progressive. The righteous shall live by his steadiness in the Word of God that was spoken, the Word of God that was written and the vision that was inspired thereof.

"…but the just shall live by his faith." Habakkuk 2:4

Why did I take you through this? I took you this way because our plans should not come out of our own self-centered desires, but out of seeking God's will for our lives.

God created us with a purpose. In His will for our lives lies the purpose for which we were created. It is in our purpose that we will please God, render the best service to mankind, find the most fulfillments and reap the greatest rewards.

Chapter Twenty

DEFINE COMPELLING REASONS

---⊕---

Foundation Scripture: Luke 19:9-10

"And <u>Jesus said unto him</u>, This day is salvation come to this house forsomuch as he also is a son of Abraham. For the Son of man is come to seek and to save that which was lost."

What is your "why?" What are your compelling reasons for doing what you plan to do?

Compelling reasons are statements that clearly explain why you are doing what you're doing. They have strong emotion and passion attached to them because they serve as the fuel for your actions.

Jesus, more than anyone, knew the importance of having compelling reasons to accomplish a goal. His reason was to fulfill the plan of God. He stated, *"For the Son of Man is come to seek and to save that which is lost."* (Matthew 18:11)

In his compelling reason, the Kingdom of God was first and foremost in his heart. His compelling reason was not self-centered. He didn't say he came to die for mankind so that he could be highly exalted and given a name above every name. On the contrary, he sought only to please God and provide his best service to mankind. He was so passionate about it that he would never quit or call on angels for help. He endured to the cross so that the plan of God might be accomplished.

Are your compelling reasons aligned with the will of God? Does it serve His purpose? Does it further the Kingdom of God? Does it provide a service to mankind? Is your compelling reason in harmony with your value system? Does it ignite your passion?

Someone once told the story of how they were in the hospital and observed a person on a life support machine. They noticed how the electronic dot on the heart monitor slid up and down across the screen creating an un-evened saw-tooth image. In an instant, The Lord revealed to them how that signified life. The ups and the downs were life. If that electronic dot always stayed up or always stayed down, the person would be dead. The very fact that we have ups and downs in life is confirmation that we are alive!

That is why it is paramount that we have clearly defined undeniable reasons for what we plan to do. Those reasons will keep us striving for the goal in the face of obstacles. Our compelling reasons will help us silence internal conflict. The last thing we need is to be conflicted about whether or not we are doing the right thing, and doing it for the right reason when we are faced with obstacles.

Imagine working hard to climb a mountain. The higher you go, the more difficult it becomes. It was nice and warm and sunny at the bottom, but it's stormy and slippery near the top. To make matters worse, the higher you go, the thinner the air gets. So now you're cold, it's stormy, visibility is low, you're hungry, thirsty, and tired. It's getting more and more slippery the higher you go and you must now use more strength to climb.

Most definitely, if you did not have compelling reasons for climbing that mountain, those combined factors would have you heading back down to the more desirable conditions at the base of the mountain. Imagine then how you would feel after quitting, when you find out that you were only three feet from the top. When times are at their worst, is not the time to quit. It is time to stretch; to reach further and commit to seeing your efforts through to the end.

I've seen it happen time and time again. A person would work hard to achieve something and get within reach of their breakthrough; then quit. They quit due to a lack of defined compelling reasons that help keep people in the game throughout any obstacle or prolonged trial.

"For the invisible things of him from the creation of the world are clearly seen, being understood by the things that are made, even his eternal power and Godhead; so that they are without excuse:" Romans 1:20

The invisible things are clearly understood by the things that are made. In other words, everything that God will do through you has had a birthplace. Just like a man has to be birthed through a woman in order to move about on the earth, so do thoughts and visions have to be birthed through the faith and actions of people in order to manifest in the physical realm.

What happens when the woman gets ready to give birth? She starts to experience labor pangs. The same thing happens when you are ready to give birth to your vision—the obstacles and difficulty that you encounter are wrenching labor pangs.

Look at the story of Hezekiah in 2 Kings 18-19 and Isaiah 36-37. The Assyrian army came and spoke to the Children of Israel and sowed fear and hopelessness in their hearts. Look at what Hezekiah said when he sent for the prophet to inquire to the Lord for help:

"And they said unto him, Thus saith Hezekiah, This day is a day of trouble, and of rebuke, and of blasphemy: for the children are come to the birth, and there is not strength to bring forth." Isaiah 37:3

In the mist of a trial, they had no strength, no faith and no joy to manifest the covenant promises of God. Therefore, intercession had to be made. Compelling reasons intercede on your behalf. They provide the strength and steadiness that is needed to go through the pangs of birth and manifest the vision that God has placed within you.

Chapter Twenty-One

IDENTIFY THE STEPS

--- ⊕ ---

Foundation Scripture: 2 Samuel 22:37

"Thou hast enlarged my steps under me; so that my feet did not slip."

In his song of praise to The Lord, David said something that was key to accomplishing a vision. He acknowledged that God enlarged his steps under him so that his feet did not slip. To *"enlarge my steps so that my feet did not slip,"* simply means to identify the steps necessary to take to accomplish our vision. To identify the steps, means that when we write the vision and make it plain, we are making it clear what must be done step by step to accomplish the vision.

Here is an example of how I identified the steps when accomplishing a vision of mine a few years ago. As a Financial Adviser, my mission was two-fold: 1. Provide my clients with a high level of personal service, and 2. Be the top producing representative in my region.

First, in order to achieve those goals, I wrote out my vision:

"Sign up 300 new clients before the end of the year."

Secondly, I defined my compelling reasons:

1. Give my clients a level of service unrivaled by any other financial adviser, and

2. Make sure I take first place when the production awards are passed out at the end of the year.

Thirdly, I identified the steps needed to accomplish my vision:

1. Write out a prayer confession that I will confess daily to give me the spiritual help needed to accomplish such a feat.

2. Write down my target list of schools in which to do presentations.

3. Identify non-work days such as student testing dates, holidays, and vacation days.

4. Make contact with the school districts and school principals to set up presentations to offer retirement plan services to the entire school staff.

5. Set aside two hours in the early evening, three days per week to make follow-up phone calls.

6. Set aside money to cover print costs, giveaways and refreshments.

7. Hire an assistant to handle the paperwork processing and client requests in our office.

8. Put together my compliance-approved power point presentation.

9. Develop an information sheet to get referrals.

10. Set up annual account review dates with existing clients.

11. Set up dates to inspect my assistant's assignments i.e. keeping a record of thank you cards sent out to every new client, applications entered correctly on the data system, files set up properly according to compliance requirements, and so on.

12. Periodically get the production bulletin to see how my peers are progressing with their production.

All that was left to do at that point was to **take action.** I followed all those steps and, by the end of the year, surpassed my vision and signed up 348 new clients. I was also distinguished as number one in the region with almost double the production of the next highest producing representative.

Results will work this way as it relates to achieving goals, completing plans, and manifesting visions, but only if you identify your steps. This process is no respecter of persons when followed without deviation—just as it worked for me, it'll work for you!

This is only one important key to manifesting the vision. There is yet another key that is just as vital: effective time management.

Chapter Twenty-Two

EFFECTIVE TIME MANAGEMENT

---------------------------------- ⊕ ----------------------------------

Foundation Scripture: Ecclesiastes 8:6

"Because to every purpose there is time and judgment, therefore the misery of man is great upon him."

To every purpose there is time or opportunity to accomplish it. Time does not stand still; it is always moving. That is why there is a dire need to maximize the time that we have and even request the Lord to help us to redeem the time that we lost.

Here is a three-step rule to help manage your time. It has worked quite effectively for me over the years, so I'm sure it can have positive results for you, as well.

1. **Envision** where you want to be or what you want to have accomplished at the end of the time period.

2. **Identify** the steps you must take in order to achieve your goal.

3. **Assign** a specific block of time to accomplish each step.

Envisioning is an important first step that must not be skipped when managing your time. Just like everything else that pertains to manifesting the unseen, it all begins with vision. You must see it before you can seize it. You must see it in your heart before you can seize it with your hands.

Next, you must identify the steps needed to achieve your goal. This will allow you to know how many tasks need to be done within a certain amount of time. This will also help you to be more realistic about what things you really can fit into your schedule and what assignments you perhaps need to start saying "no" to.

Once you know your workload, assigning that work to specific blocks of time brings it to a manageable level where it can be completed. If you don't do this step, you will find yourself wasting precious time—time that is needed to accomplish other things.

I have a saying that goes, "All spirituality has practical application." Therefore, the principles in this book are spiritual and they will work if you apply them. Let me give you an example of implementing this three-step rule to effective time management so you can start applying it to *your* schedule.

I would start by asking myself, and then envisioning, where I want to be by the end of the month. Just like me, you will find yourself tackling quite a few areas of interests simultaneously. For instance, the areas I manage my time for are: finances, writing my book, supporting the Kingdom of God, spending time with my wife, spending time with my children, spiritual growth, healthy diet and exercise.

Once I envision where I want to be, I identify the steps of each goal or purpose.

Spiritual Growth:

1. Write down five to ten things that happened today that I am thankful to God for.

2. Take a few minutes daily to pray for others.

3. Pray for at least an hour daily.

4. Find a scripture to meditate.

5. Confess (Read aloud) the scriptures that remind me of God's promises.

6. I must read at least an hour daily.

Time with my wife:

1. Schedule a date night.

2. Schedule any activities that we must attend together.

3. Schedule prayer time together.

4. Schedule a phone call during the work day.

5. Leave schedule open during some evenings for "hang out" time.

Time with my children:

1. I must schedule them in before I schedule anything else.

2. Plan activities for us to enjoy together.

3. Have morning devotion with them twice weekly.

Finances:

1. Write down what I need to cover my basic needs.

2. Write down what I want to bring in over and above my needs.

3. I must schedule telephone time to prospect for clients.

4. I must schedule time to see clients.

5. I must make fifteen calls three days per week and keep eight appointments per week.

Supporting the Kingdom of God:

1. I determined what I will give in addition to my tithe and will work to obtain the gift.

Healthy diet and exercise:

1. I will schedule five exercise periods per week.

2. I will plan my meals the night before each day.

Write my book:

1. I must schedule time to write daily.

Those are the steps that I must take to manifest what I have envisioned.

Here is a schedule according to the steps:

4:30am-5: 55am Wake up-prayer, meditation on the Word of God, confessions, read the Bible.

5:55am-6am Visualize my day.

6am-6:20am Wake up kids. Morning devotions.

6:20am-7:30am Shower, get dressed, have breakfast.

7:30am-8am Drop kids off at school.

8am-8:45am Drive to the office or an appointment.

9:00am-12noon If in the office, make prospecting calls to schedule appointments and return calls. If in the field on appointments, be sure to obtain referrals.

12:00noon-1pm Lunch with wife.

1pm-2:30pm Call referrals to schedule appointments or attend previously scheduled appointments.

3:15pm-4:30pm Pick up kids and help them with homework.

4:30pm-5:30pm Dinner with wife and kids.

5:30pm-6:30pm Travel to Karate class.

6:30pm-7:30pm Children's Karate class

7:30pm-8:30pm Adult Karate class

8:30pm-9:00pm Travel home, Eat a light snack

9:00pm-9:30pm Bedtime for kids. Plan meals with wife for the next day. Make sure all blocks of time are assigned for the next day.

9:30pm-10:55pm Write book.

10:55pm-11:15pm Confessions, prayer, bedtime.

If you've noticed, there is not much time for television (although I do get distracted sometimes by my wife's television shows).

This is a typical Tuesday and Thursday. Everyday is not like this. On the evenings that I don't travel to karate class, I am hanging out with my wife and kids. I do schedule personal time, and some days I don't go to bed as late. But as you can see, much can be accomplished in every area if you assign specific blocks of time to the completion of the task.

Once you are successful with planning your week, start planning your month. Then plan each quarter—ninety days. With some consistency, you'll become efficient at planning your one-year, five-year and even ten-year activities, as planning your year works the same as planning your week. It really is a simple process.

When you plan your year, assign specific steps to be completed within specific months. One step might take one month or one and a half months to complete. For example, if you have identified ten steps to achieve what you have envisioned for the year, the third step might be assigned the month of March, or from March 1st –April 15th to complete.

Once you have the big picture—your vision—written for the year, and the steps identified and assigned to specific blocks of time, then your focus should be to plan from event to event. Thinking from event to event is actually just putting it in terms of step by step. When done properly, this will keep you focused and prevent you from becoming overwhelmed.

"For precept must be upon precept, precept upon precept; line upon line, line upon line; here a little, and there a little:" Isaiah 28:10

Since thinking from step to step and moving step by step is basically how we learn and prepare things in life, this method makes it much simpler to accomplish goals. If you ever watch a building being constructed, it's done in the same manner. The bottom floor is built first and then the workers stand on the newly built floor to build the second floor and so on.

Every ninety days, you should evaluate yourself to see if you are on target with accomplishing your vision for the year. If you are on target, great! If you are behind schedule, then you may want to identify resources of people who might be willing to pitch in and help you.

Chapter Twenty-Three

DILIGENCE VS. TOILING

———————— ⊕ ————————

Foundation Scripture: Ecclesiastes 9:10

"Whatsoever thy hand findeth to do, do it with thy might; for there is no work, nor device, nor knowledge, nor wisdom, in the grave, whither thou goest."

I came across this scripture during my devotions while serving as Regional Vice President for a financial service firm. I thought that it meant to put my all into my work and so I did, only to watch my life fall apart and my income decrease. Since then, I have learned a very powerful truth: when you believe that you are following God's Word and have given your efforts a chance to compound, but instead of getting better things get worse, check your revelation of the scriptures you're standing on.

Scriptures are guaranteed to work 100% of the time. Not just in the literal sense either, as we read about the first reference to work found in Genesis Chapter 2. The Lord put ADAM in the Garden of Eden to dress it and to keep it.

"And the LORD God took the man, and put him into the Garden of Eden to dress it and to keep it." Genesis 2:15

The name "ADAM" means "a suitable form or image in the likeness of God." The phrase *"and put him into the Garden of Eden,"* is more accurately translated, *"and caused him to rest into the Garden of Eden."*

Therefore, this verse should read like this: *"And The Lord God took His own image that He made in His own likeness, which was ADAM, and caused him to rest in the Garden of Eden, to serve and nurture it and to put a hedge up to protect it."*

When I discovered this, my questions were plentiful. Why was it written this way in the Hebrew language? What did it mean God caused him to rest? Why did God want him to serve and nurture the Garden as a husbandman? What was he to protect, and why was he to protect it? The answers to these questions give us the foundation of what "work" was designed to be in the life of the believer.

What did it mean that God caused him to rest?

When God caused ADAM to rest, He did not cause ADAM's body to recline in a relaxed state. If that were the case, he wouldn't have been able to tend the Garden. Instead, when God caused ADAM to rest, He caused him to cease from mental exertion, which means that ADAM did not have to try to figure things out. Everything that ADAM needed to speak and act on came by revelation from God.

Why did God want him to serve and nurture the Garden as a husbandman?

The Bible says that God planted the Garden (Genesis 2:8). When anything is planted, it is planted with the intent to grow. The fact that it was planted eastward (in the fore part of the earth) means that it was planted with the intent of it growing to cover the whole earth.

God wanted ADAM to serve the purpose of something larger than himself, with the intent of cultivating and nurturing it to grow. Notice that God doesn't call work service. He calls service work. **If your work is not service to a cause greater than you, it is not work, it is toil.** Work is only work when it is service to a cause that is greater than you.

To toil, means to overwork in such a manner that it brings about pain, fatigue and weariness of the body and the mind. It is toil that oppresses the body and mind.

Service to a cause that is greater than us does not oppress the body and mind, but on the contrary, the body and mind is liberated. Why? We are liberated because we are in line with the will of God; God's will is that we work as a service, because service is an expression of love. It is an action that is not self-centered. In service, there is provision for the server.

Why are we not to toil? We shouldn't toil because toiling is associated with the curse.

"And he called his name Noah, saying, This same shall comfort us concerning our work and toil of our hands, because of the ground which the LORD hath cursed." Genesis 5:29

We are not to toil because we have been redeemed from the curse.

"Christ hath redeemed us from the curse of the law, being made a curse for us: for it is written, Cursed is every one that hangeth on a tree:" Galatians 3:13

In Matthew Chapter 6, Jesus reveals that we are to toil no longer, but instead go back to working the way that work was originally designed. In doing so, there is provision for the server.

"And why take ye thought for raiment? Consider the lilies of the field, how they grow; they toil not, neither do they spin: And yet I say unto you, That even Solomon in all his glory was not arrayed like one of these. Wherefore, if God so clothe the grass of the field, which today is, and tomorrow is cast into the oven, shall he not much more clothe you, O ye of little faith? Therefore take no thought, saying, What shall we eat? or, What shall we drink? or, Wherewithal shall we be clothed? (For after all these things do the Gentiles seek:) for your heavenly Father knoweth that ye have need of all these things. But seek ye first the kingdom of God, and his righteousness; and all these things shall be added unto you." Matthew 6:28-31

What was he to protect, and why was he to protect it?

The word "keep" in Genesis 2:15 means to protect it or more accurately to put a hedge (of thorns) around it to protect it. ADAM was to protect the integrity of the Garden.

Why was he to protect it? He was to protect the integrity of the Garden because in the Garden was the sustaining of his life and the fulfillment of his purpose. Satan was already a thief in the earth trying to steal ADAM's authority and dominion, kill ADAM and his wife, and destroy the earth which the Garden of Eden was supposed to cover. (John 10:10.)

What is meant by the integrity of the Garden? The integrity of the Garden was ADAM's rest, ADAM's work, and ADAM's relationships. ADAM's rest— his ceasing from mental exertion. ADAM's work—his service to his God-given purpose that was greater than himself. ADAM's relationships—his relationship with God and his relationship with his wife.

Okay. Now that we understand this, let's return to the foundation scripture:

"Whatsoever thy hand findeth to do, do it with thy might; for there is no work, nor device, nor knowledge, nor wisdom, in the grave, whither thou goest." Ecclesiastes 9:10

Let's focus on the first part of that verse: "Whatsoever thy hand findeth to do, do it with thy might."

"Whatsoever" comes from a Hebrew word that means "all" or "every." "Hand" means "power" or "ability." "Findeth" means "to be present or to be in the moment." "Might" means "power produced from strong inner desire," it can be simply stated as "passion."

So the verse should read like this: *"Everything (all that pertains to your life) that you are present and in the moment to do, do it with passion, pouring all your desire into its accomplishment;"*

I originally thought that this verse meant for me to focus entirely on work, but it doesn't. It means to be diligent in all that pertains to your life. Diligence means steady application in the business at hand. It is the opposite of slack or sloth, which is the relaxing of the hands.

There are three sections of life: rest, work, and relationships. Rest— ceasing from mental exertion, which keeps you healthy. Work–service in your God-given purpose, which contributes to the progression of mankind and economically sustains your life. Relationships with people—adds fulfillment to life. Relationships with God–adds joy, peace, and happiness to a person's heart.

When I focused my entire life on my work, my relationships suffered. My life basically began to fall apart. That happened because I did not protect the integrity of my life through being diligent to keep myself balanced.

"A false balance is abomination to the LORD: but a just weight is his delight." Proverbs 11:1

This scripture speaks to a business transaction; whereas, the scales have been manipulated so that the person who manipulated them would receive more money than he should. This is an abomination to the Lord because it speaks falsehood and offends God. It speaks falsehood because the person who is doing the defrauding is created in God's image.

So the defrauder's actions are saying, "This is how God acts, in whose image I was created. I do as He does," which is an abomination because God cannot lie nor cheat. This very much offends God. To defraud another person is to defraud the Lord because the person defrauded was created in God's image as well.

God revealed to me that life is a business transaction. We trade time for gain. But God doesn't want our gain to be unbalanced. Balance begets increase; lack of balance will produce sorrow and regret. Again, our life has three sections: 1) Rest—health, 2) Work--economic stability and 3) Relationships–happiness, joy, peace, and fulfillment. If there is any lack in any of these areas you are considered poor.

If a man has money and good health, but no relationships; people would say, "oh that poor man." If a man has money and relationships, but bad health; people would say, "oh that poor man." If a man has relationships and good health, but no money; people would say, "oh that poor man." But God wants us rich. Jesus became poor, that through His poverty, we might be rich. (2 Corinthians 8:9)

"Divers weights and divers measures, both of them are alike abomination to the LORD." Proverbs 20:10

Weights are levels of passion. Measures are duration of time. God wants us to be diligent and steady. He wants us to have the same standard of passion and time devoted to each section of our life. Where there is no balance, there is a lack of integrity. The principle of balance is integrity.

"Let me be weighed in an even balance, that God may know mine integrity."
Job 31:6

In order to keep a balanced life, we must master "being in the moment." In the very moment of what we find ourselves doing, we must commit the same high standard of passion and quality of time that we do in other areas of life. We are responsible for getting the proper rest, doing our work with excellence, and relating to one another with the same weights and measures that we put into our work and sleep.

Order always comes before increase in the Kingdom of God and the way one thinks always precedes the way one acts. If you will diligently practice the principles explained in this book, every area in your life will experience a new godly order and godly increase with no sorrow. As you confess, meditate, and observe to do God's Word, your thoughts will change, which will in turn change your actions. You will notice a marked difference in your life in three to six months if you are consistent. Once you start doing the right things, the results don't take long to manifest.

Making your way prosperous is accomplished by the right actions—God's way of doing things. The right actions are produced by the right thoughts—God's way of thinking. The right thoughts are produced by hearing the right words—God's Words, which you can increase your frequency of hearing through confession and meditation.

Part V - Action Points

When I was younger I took a spiritual gift assessment offered by Team Ministry (http://www.Teamministry.com) which gave me clarity on my spiritual gifts. After discovering the spiritual gifts I possessed, the frustration was over. I no longer wondered why I couldn't play sports as well as my friends or why I felt so strongly about certain things. God created me with a clear purpose in mind and He wired me to operate a certain way.

Many people are angry and frustrated with life and don't know the real reasons why. It is because they are not doing what they were designed to do nor living the life they were designed to live. Take a spiritual gift assessment then align your goals and desires around those gifts. You will discover a life of greater meaning; one that honors God and provides the greatest benefit to mankind that you could render. You will also find great satisfaction and peace and you will never struggle financially. Working your spiritual gifts will sustain your life. Your spiritual gifts will provide for you in greater measure than anything else. They will bring you riches in every area of life with no sorrow.

1. What is your vision? What are you passionate about? What are your spiritual gifts?

_____

_____

_____

_____

_____

2. What are your compelling reasons for your vision? What reasons will compel you to move forward toward your goal in the mist of gut-wrenching adversity? Are they compelling enough to steer you away from distractions?

_____

_____

_____

_____

_____

3. Nobody knows you better than you! Write down all of your potential distractions. Then next to each distraction, write down what you will do specifically to steer away from them.

_____

_____

_____

_____

_____

4. Identify the steps. What specific steps will you take to get from where you are to achieve your goals and accomplish your vision? Sometimes the steps I need to take are not always clear to me in the beginning. God promised to enlarge my steps, which means to make it clear what to do next so that when I take a step, my feet won't slip. *"Thou hast enlarged my steps under me; so that my feet did not slip."* 2 Samuel 22:37. In the morning while meditating scriptures, I simply ask, "Lord, what do I do next? Make it clear to me what steps to take." Then, I simply trust that He has answered my prayer and I write down the thoughts as they come to me throughout the day. (It is very important to write the thoughts as you receive them. Do not filter them through your thinking. Many times they either won't make sense initially or they will be incredibly simple. Just write them down before you forget the exact words.)

_____

_____

_____

_____

_____

5. Effective time management. Simply picture each hour as a train car and fill each train car with a task. Be careful not to overload your train car. It is okay to have an empty train car from time to time to allow for completing incomplete tasks. Once the next hour is here, you must be on to the tasks in the next train car. Live in the moment and put all of your effort and focus into completing the task at hand. Focus and don't allow thoughts of previous or future task to overwhelm you.

Doing it this way will enable you to accomplish more in your day. It will also help you to mentally move on to the next task at the turn of the hour. Mentally moving on to the next task is important because if you can discipline yourself to leave a task and move on to the next one, you can discipline yourself to leave work at work when it is time to spend time with family.

_____

_____

_____

_____

_____

6. Write three specific adjustments you will make to create balance in your life?

Our day can easily be divided up into three main categories: Work, Relationships and Rest.

_____

_____

_____

_____

_____

Additional Notes

A Golden Opportunity

---------------- ⊕ ----------------

One day, the Lord gave me a revelation into the hearts of mankind when a situation arose with my eldest son. I told him that he could no longer watch television, except for certain Christian and Public Broadcasting stations. He asked me why, and I explained that it wasn't punishment for something he had done, but instead it was because I desired to see his behavior change.

Of course, he didn't understand. He and his siblings murmured like the children of Israel in the wilderness about that television, but I remained steadfast in my decision.

A few weeks later, he came to me and told me that I was right. He asked me how I knew that their behavior would change. I told him that the Lord revealed to me that our negative behavior is the result of the negative seeds planted in our heart through vision and hearing i.e. certain television and radio programming.

My son murmured and complained and sometimes disobeyed because his finite mind could not fathom why I would demand such a change, but he now understands that it was for his good and his behavior is better because of it. There was such a sudden positive change in his behavior that one of his teachers called me personally to applaud me for whatever I was doing at home that seemed to be working.

God is the same way. He knows that no man is truly rich unless he is born again.

People want to take their own paths to what they believe to be right for themselves. However, like my son, their finite minds cannot fathom why The All-Knowing God has structured salvation a certain way, and if any man's soul would be saved from eternal damnation, it has to be done God's way.

The first man, ADAM, disobeyed God and sinned. As a result, sin passed from ADAM unto all men. Whether we are a sinner or not, is not an issue of behavior, but an issue of how we were born. We all were born in sin and therefore need to be born again unto eternal life through Jesus Christ our Lord.

The first step is to repent and then be baptized in the Name of Jesus for the remission of sins, and then you shall receive the gift of the Holy Ghost (Holy Spirit).

"Then Peter said unto them, Repent, and be baptized every one of you in the name of Jesus Christ for the remission of sins, and ye shall receive the gift of the Holy Ghost." Acts 2:38

"That if thou shalt confess with thy mouth the Lord Jesus, and shalt believe in thine heart that God hath raised him from the dead, thou shalt be saved. For with the heart man believeth unto righteousness; and with the mouth confession is made unto salvation. For the Scripture saith, Whosoever believeth on him shall not be ashamed." Romans 10:9-11

"For there is no difference between the Jew and the Greek: for the same Lord over all is rich unto all that call upon him. For whosoever shall call upon the name of the Lord shall be saved." Romans 10:12-13

If you are not saved, please join me in confessing the following prayer aloud:

"Father, your Word says that if I confess that Jesus Christ is Lord, and believe in my heart that you have raised him from the dead, I shall be saved. Therefore, Father, I ask Jesus to come into my heart right now and be The Lord of my life. I confess that Jesus Christ is Lord and believe in my heart that you have raised him from the dead. I repent of my sins and renounce my past. Thank you for forgiveness and for saving my soul, in Jesus' Name, Amen."

Praise God! If you prayed this prayer aloud and meant what you prayed, then you are saved right now.

It is now necessary that you go to a local church that teaches the Word of God and get Baptized in Jesus' Name, and you shall receive the gift of the Holy Ghost.

Read the Bible for yourself that you may learn of all the wonderful promises God has given to us who believe on Him through Jesus Christ.

Congratulations on taking advantage of this golden opportunity.

May God bless you indeed!

Confession and Meditation Scriptures

Prosperity

Genesis 1:26-28

And God said, Let us make man in our image, after our likeness: and let them have dominion over the fish of the sea, and over the fowl of the air, and over the cattle, and over all the earth, and over every creeping thing that creepeth upon the earth. So God created man in his *own* image, in the image of God created he him; male and female created he them. And God blessed them, and God said unto them, Be fruitful, and multiply, and replenish the earth, and subdue it: and have dominion over the fish of the sea, and over the fowl of the air, and over every living thing that moveth upon the earth.

Genesis 8:22

While the earth remaineth, seedtime and harvest, and cold and heat, and summer and winter, and day and night shall not cease.

Genesis 12:3

Now the LORD had said unto Abram, Get thee out of thy country, and from thy kindred, and from thy father's house, unto a land that I will shew thee: And I will make of thee a great nation, and I will bless thee, and make thy name great; and thou shalt be a blessing: And I will bless them that bless thee, and curse him that curseth thee: and in thee shall all families of the earth be blessed.

Genesis 13:2

And Abram *was* very rich in cattle, in silver, and in gold.

Galatians 3:13-14

Christ hath redeemed us from the curse of the law, being made a curse for us: for it is written, Cursed *is* every one that hangeth on a tree: That the blessing of Abraham might come on the Gentiles through Jesus Christ; that we might receive the promise of the Spirit through faith.

Galatians 3:29

And if ye *be* Christ's, then are ye Abraham's seed, and heirs according to the promise.

Genesis 26:12-14

Then Isaac sowed in that land, and received in the same year an hundredfold: and the LORD blessed him. And the man waxed great, and went forward, and grew until he became very great: For he had possession of flocks, and possession of herds, and great store of servants: and the Philistines envied him.

Genesis 39:2-3

And the LORD was with Joseph, and he was a prosperous man; and he was in the house of his master the Egyptian. And his master saw that the LORD *was* with him, and that the LORD made all that he did to prosper in his hand.

Genesis 41:33-36

Now therefore let Pharaoh look out a man discreet and wise, and set him over the land of Egypt. Let Pharaoh do *this,* and let him appoint officers over the land, and take up the fifth part of the land of Egypt in the seven plenteous years. And let them gather all the food of those good years that come, and lay up corn under the hand of Pharaoh, and let them keep food in the cities. And that food shall be for store to the land against the seven years of famine, which shall be in the land of Egypt; that the land perish not through the famine.

Exodus 23:22-25

But if thou shalt indeed obey his voice, and do all that I speak; then I will be an enemy unto thine enemies , and an adversary unto thine adversaries. For mine Angel shall go before thee, and bring thee in unto the Amorites, and the Hittites, and the Perizzites, and the Canaanites, the Hivites, and the Jebusites: and I will cut them off. Thou shalt not bow down to their gods, nor serve them, nor do after their works: but thou shalt utterly overthrow them, and quite break down their images. And ye shall serve the LORD your God, and he shall bless thy bread, and thy water; and I will take sickness away from the midst of thee.

Leviticus 26:3-12

If ye walk in my statutes, and keep my commandments, and do them; Then I will give you rain in due season, and the land shall yield her increase, and the trees of the field shall yield their fruit. And your threshing shall reach unto the vintage, and the vintage shall reach unto the sowing time: and ye shall eat your bread to the full, and dwell in your land safely. And I will give peace in the land, and ye shall lie down, and none shall make *you* afraid: and I will rid evil beasts out of the land, neither shall the sword go through your land. And ye shall chase your enemies, and they shall fall before you by the sword. And five of you shall chase an hundred, and an hundred of you shall put ten thousand to flight: and your enemies shall fall before you by the sword. For I will have respect unto you, and make you fruitful, and multiply you, and establish my covenant with you. And ye shall eat old store, and bring forth the old because of the new. And I will set my tabernacle among you: and my soul shall not abhor you. And I will walk among you, and will be your God, and ye shall be my people.

Deuteronomy 1:11

The LORD God of your fathers make you a thousand times so many more as ye *are,* and bless you, as he hath promised you!

Deuteronomy 6:10-12

And it shall be, when the LORD thy God shall have brought thee into the land which he sware unto thy fathers, to Abraham, to Isaac, and to Jacob, to give thee great and goodly cities, which thou buildedst not, And houses full of all good *things,* which thou filledst not, and wells digged, which thou diggedst not, vineyards and olive trees, which thou plantedst not; when thou shalt have eaten and be full; *Then* beware lest thou forget the LORD, which brought thee forth out of the land of Egypt, from the house of bondage.

Deuteronomy 11:13-15

And it shall come to pass, if ye shall hearken diligently unto my commandments which I command you this day, to love the LORD your God, and to serve him with all your heart and with all your soul, That I will give *you* the rain of your land in his due season, the first rain and the latter rain, that thou mayest gather in thy corn, and thy wine, and thine oil. And I will send grass in thy fields for thy cattle, that thou mayest eat and be full.

Deuteronomy 28:1-13

And it shall come to pass, if thou shalt hearken diligently unto the voice of the LORD thy God, to observe *and* to do all his commandments which I command thee this day, that the LORD thy God will set thee on high above all nations of the earth: And all these blessings shall come on thee, and overtake thee, if thou shalt hearken unto the voice of the LORD thy God. Blessed *shalt* thou *be* in the city, and blessed *shalt* thou *be* in the field. Blessed *shall be* the fruit of thy body, and the fruit of thy ground, and the fruit of thy cattle, the increase of thy kine, and the flocks of thy sheep. Blessed *shall be* thy basket and thy store. Blessed *shalt* thou *be* when thou comest in, and blessed *shalt* thou *be* when thou goest out. The LORD shall cause thine enemies that rise up against thee to be smitten before thy face: they shall come out against thee one way, and flee before thee seven ways. The LORD shall command the blessing upon thee in thy storehouses, and in all that thou settest thine hand unto; and he shall bless thee in the land which the LORD thy God giveth thee. The LORD shall establish thee an holy people unto himself, as he hath sworn unto thee, if thou shalt keep the commandments of the LORD thy God, and walk in his ways. And all people of the earth shall see that thou art called by the name of the LORD; and they shall be afraid of thee. And the LORD shall make thee plenteous in goods, in the fruit of thy body, and in the fruit of thy cattle, and in the fruit of thy ground, in the land which the LORD sware unto thy fathers to give thee. The LORD shall open unto thee his good treasure, the heaven to give the rain unto thy land in his season, and to bless all the work of thine hand: and thou shalt lend unto many nations, and thou shalt not borrow. And the LORD shall make thee the head, and not the tail; and thou shalt be above only, and thou shalt not be beneath; if that thou hearken unto the commandments of the LORD thy God, which I command thee this day, to observe and to do *them:*

Deuteronomy 33:19

They shall call the people unto the mountain; there they shall offer sacrifices of righteousness: for they shall suck *of* the abundance of the seas, and *of* treasures hid in the sand.

Job 22:21-28

Acquaint now thyself with him, and be at peace: thereby good shall come unto thee. Receive, I pray thee, the law from his mouth, and lay up his words in thine heart. If thou return to the Almighty, thou shalt be built up, thou shalt put away iniquity far from thy tabernacles. Then shalt thou lay up gold as dust, and the *gold* of Ophir as the stones of the brooks. Yea, the Almighty shall be thy defence, and thou shalt have plenty of silver. For then shalt thou have thy delight in the Almighty, and shalt lift up thy face unto God.

Thou shalt make thy prayer unto him, and he shall hear thee, and thou shalt pay thy vows. Thou shalt also decree a thing, and it shall be established unto thee: and the light shall shine upon thy ways.

Psalm 1:1-3

Blessed *is* the man that walketh not in the counsel of the ungodly, nor standeth in the way of sinners, nor sitteth in the seat of the scornful. But his delight *is* in the law of the LORD; and in his law doth he meditate day and night. And he shall be like a tree planted by the rivers of water, that bringeth forth his fruit in his season; his leaf also shall not wither; and whatsoever he doeth shall prosper.

Psalm 37:3-5

Trust in the LORD, and do good; *so* shalt thou dwell in the land, and verily thou shalt be fed. Delight thyself also in the LORD; and he shall give thee the desires of thine heart. Commit thy way unto the LORD; trust also in him; and he shall bring *it* to pass.

Psalm 37:25

I have been young, and *now* am old; yet have I not seen the righteous forsaken, nor his seed begging bread.

Psalm 85:12

Yea, the LORD shall give *that which is* good; and our land shall yield her increase.

Psalm 112:1-3

Praise ye the LORD. Blessed *is* the man *that* feareth the LORD, *that* delighteth greatly in his commandments. His seed shall be mighty upon earth: the generation of the upright shall be blessed. Wealth and riches *shall be* in his house: and his righteousness endureth for ever.

Psalm 115:14

The LORD shall increase you more and more, you and your children.

Proverbs 3:9-10

Honour the LORD with thy substance, and with the firstfruits of all thine increase: So shall thy barns be filled with plenty, and thy presses shall burst out with new wine.

Proverbs 10:4

He becometh poor that dealeth *with* a slack hand: but the hand of the diligent maketh rich.

Proverbs 10:22

The blessing of the LORD, it maketh rich, and he addeth no sorrow with it.

Proverbs 13:22

A good *man* leaveth an inheritance to his children's children: and the wealth of the sinner *is* laid up for the just.

Proverbs 15:6

In the house of the righteous *is* much treasure: but in the revenues of the wicked is trouble.

Proverbs 22:6-7

Train up a child in the way he should go: and when he is old, he will not depart from it. The rich ruleth over the poor, and the borrower *is* servant to the lender.

Proverbs 24:27

Prepare thy work without, and make it fit for thyself in the field; and afterwards build thine house.

Proverbs 27:12

A prudent *man* foreseeth the evil, *and* hideth himself; *but* the simple pass on, *and* are punished.

Proverbs 27:23

Be thou diligent to know the state of thy flocks, *and* look well to thy herds.

Ecclesiastes 5:18-19

Behold *that* which I have seen: *it is* good and comely *for one* to eat and to drink, and to enjoy the good of all his labour that he taketh under the sun all the days of his life, which God giveth him: for it *is* his portion. Every man also to whom God hath given riches and wealth, and hath given him power to eat thereof, and to take his portion, and to rejoice in his labour; this *is* the gift of God.

Isaiah 1:19

If ye be willing and obedient, ye shall eat the good of the land:

Isaiah 48:17-18

Thus saith the LORD, thy Redeemer, the Holy One of Israel; I *am* the LORD thy God which teacheth thee to profit, which leadeth thee by the way *that* thou shouldest go. O that thou hadst hearkened to my commandments! Then had thy peace been as a river, and thy righteousness as the waves of the sea:

Isaiah 49:10

They shall not hunger nor thirst; neither shall the heat nor sun smite them: for he that hath mercy on them shall lead them, even by the springs of water shall he guide them.

Jeremiah 29:11

I know the plans that I have for you, declares the LORD. They are plans for peace and not disaster, plans to give you a future filled with hope.

Joel 2:23-26

Be glad then, ye children of Zion, and rejoice in the LORD your God: for he hath given you the former rain moderately, and he will cause to come down for you the rain, the former rain, and the latter rain in the first *month*. And the floors shall be full of wheat, and the fats shall overflow with wine and oil. And I will restore to you the years that the locust hath eaten, the cankerworm, and the caterpillar, and the palmerworm, my great army which I sent among you. And ye shall eat in plenty, and be satisfied, and praise the name of the LORD your God, that hath dealt wondrously with you: and my people shall never be ashamed.

Matthew 6:31-33

Therefore take no thought, saying, What shall we eat? or, What shall we drink? or, Wherewithal shall we be clothed? (For after all these things do the Gentiles seek:) for your heavenly Father knoweth that ye have need of all these things. But seek ye first the kingdom of God, and his righteousness; and all these things shall be added unto you.

Matthew 7:7-11

Ask, and it shall be given you; seek, and ye shall find; knock, and it shall be opened unto you. For every one that asketh receiveth; and he that seeketh findeth; and to him that knocketh it shall be opened. Or what man is there of you, whom if his son ask bread, will he give him a stone? Or if he ask a fish, will he give him a serpent? If ye then, being evil, know how to give good gifts unto your children, how much more shall your Father which is in heaven give good things to them that ask him?

Mark 10:28-30

Then Peter began to say unto him, Lo, we have left all, and have followed thee. And Jesus answered and said, Verily I say unto you, There is no man that hath left house, or brethren, or sisters, or father, or mother, or wife, or children, or lands, for my sake, and the gospel's, But he shall receive an hundredfold now in this time, houses, and brethren, and sisters, and mothers, and children, and lands, with persecutions; and in the world to come eternal life.

Mark 4:14-29

The sower soweth the word. And these are they by the way side, where the word is sown; but when they have heard, Satan cometh immediately, and taketh away the word that was sown in their hearts. And these are they likewise which are sown on stony ground; who, when they have heard the word, immediately receive it with gladness; And have no root in themselves, and so endure but for a time: afterward, when affliction or persecution ariseth for the word's sake, immediately they are offended. And these are they which are sown among thorns; such as hear the word, And the cares of this world, and the deceitfulness of riches, and the lusts of other things entering in, choke the word, and it becometh unfruitful. And these are they which are sown on good ground; such as hear the word, and receive *it,* and bring forth fruit, some thirtyfold, some sixty, and some an hundred. And he said unto them, Is a candle brought to be put under a bushel, or under a bed? And not to be set on a candlestick? For there is nothing hid, which shall not be manifested; neither was any thing kept secret, but that it should come abroad. If any man have ears to hear, let him hear. And he said unto them, Take heed what ye hear: with what measure ye mete, it shall be measured to you: and unto you that hear shall more be given. For he that hath, to him shall be given: and he that hath not, from him shall be taken even that which he hath. And he said, So is the kingdom of God, as if a man should cast seed into the ground; And should sleep, and rise night and day, and the seed should spring and grow up, he knoweth not how. For the earth bringeth forth fruit of herself; first the blade, then the ear, after that the full corn in the ear. But when the fruit is brought forth, immediately he putteth in the sickle, because the harvest is come.

John 10:10

The thief cometh not, but for to steal, and to kill, and to destroy: I am come that they might have life, and that they might have *it* more abundantly.

Romans 8:32

He that spared not his own Son, but delivered him up for us all, how shall he not with him also freely give us all things?

1 Corinthians 3:21-23

Therefore let no man glory in men. For all things are yours; Whether Paul, or Apollos, or Cephas, or the world, or life, or death, or things present, or things to come; all are yours; And ye are Christ's; and Christ *is* God's.

2 Corinthians 8:7-9

Therefore, as ye abound in every *thing, in* faith, and utterance, and knowledge, and *in* all diligence, and *in* your love to us, *see* that ye abound in this grace also.I speak not by commandment, but by occasion of the forwardness of others, and to prove the sincerity of your love. For ye know the grace of our Lord Jesus Christ, that, though he was rich, yet for your sakes he became poor, that ye through his poverty might be rich.

2 Corinthians 9:6-11

But this *I say,* He which soweth sparingly shall reap also sparingly; and he which soweth bountifully shall reap also bountifully. Every man according as he purposeth in his heart, *so let him give;* not grudgingly, or of necessity: for God loveth a cheerful giver. And God *is* able to make all grace abound toward you; that ye, always having all sufficiency in all *things,* may abound to every good work: (As it is written, He hath dispersed abroad; he hath given to the poor: his righteousness remaineth for ever. Now he that ministereth seed to the sower both minister bread for *your* food, and multiply your seed sown, and increase the fruits of your righteousness;) Being enriched in everything to all bountifulness, which causeth through us thanksgiving to God.

2 Thessalonians 3:10-14

For even when we were with you, this we commanded you, that if any would not work, neither should he eat. For we hear that there are some which walk among you disorderly, working not at all, but are busybodies. Now them that are such we command and exhort by our Lord Jesus Christ, that with quietness they work, and eat their own bread. But ye, brethren, be not weary in well doing. And if any man obey not our word by this epistle, note that man, and have no company with him, that he may be ashamed.

James 1:17

Every good gift and every perfect gift is from above, and cometh down from the Father of lights, with whom is no variableness, neither shadow of turning.

3 John 2

Beloved, I wish above all things that thou mayest prosper and be in health, even as thy soul prospereth.

Meditation

Genesis 24:63

And Isaac went out to meditate in the field at the eventide: and he lifted up his eyes, and saw, and, behold, the camels *were* coming.

Joshua 1:8

This book of the law shall not depart out of thy mouth; but thou shalt meditate therein day and night, that thou mayest observe to do according to all that is written therein: for then thou shalt make thy way prosperous, and then thou shalt have good success.

Psalm 1:2

But his delight *is* in the law of the LORD; and in his law doth he meditate day and night.

Psalm 63:6

When I remember thee upon my bed, *and* meditate on thee in the *night* watches.

Psalm 77:12

I will meditate also of all thy work, and talk of thy doings.

Psalm 119:15

I will meditate in thy precepts, and have respect unto thy ways.

Psalm 119:23

Princes also did sit *and* speak against me: *but* thy servant did meditate in thy statutes.

Psalm 119:48

My hands also will I lift up unto thy commandments, which I have loved; and I will meditate in thy statutes.

Psalm 119:78

Let the proud be ashamed; for they dealt perversely with me without a cause: *but* I will meditate in thy precepts.

Psalm 119:130

The entrance of thy words giveth light; it giveth understanding unto the simple.

Psalm 119:148

Mine eyes prevent the *night* watches, that I might meditate in thy word.

Psalm 143:5

I remember the days of old; I meditate on all thy works; I muse on the work of thy hands.

John 15:7

If ye abide in me, and my words abide in you, ye shall ask what ye will, and it shall be done unto you.

1 Timothy 4:15

Meditate upon these things; give thyself wholly to them; that thy profiting may appear to all.

Giving

Genesis 14:18-20

And Melchizedek king of Salem brought forth bread and wine: and he *was* the priest of the most high God. And he blessed him, and said, Blessed *be* Abram of the most high God, possessor of heaven and earth: And blessed be the most high God, which hath delivered thine enemies into thy hand. And he gave him tithes of all.

Exodus 23:19-22

The first of the firstfruits of thy land thou shalt bring into the house of the LORD thy God. Thou shalt not seethe a kid in his mother's milk. Behold, I send an Angel before thee, to keep thee in the way, and to bring thee into the place which I have prepared. Beware of him, and obey his voice, provoke him not; for he will not pardon your transgressions: for my name *is* in him. But if thou shalt indeed obey his voice, and do all that I speak; then I will be an enemy unto thine enemies, and an adversary unto thine adversaries.

Leviticus 27:30

And all the tithe of the land, *whether* of the seed of the land, *or* of the fruit of the tree, *is* the LORD'S: *it is* holy unto the LORD.

Deuteronomy 14:22

Thou shalt truly tithe all the increase of thy seed, that the field bringeth forth year by year.

Psalm 41:1

Blessed *is* he that considereth the poor: the LORD will deliver him in time of trouble.

Proverbs 3:9-10

Honour the LORD with thy substance, and with the firstfruits of all thine increase:

So shall thy barns be filled with plenty, and thy presses shall burst out with new wine.

Proverbs 11:24-25

There is that scattereth, and yet increaseth; and *there is* that withholdeth more than is meet, but *it tendeth* to poverty. The liberal soul shall be made fat: and he that watereth shall be watered also himself.

Proverbs 28:27

He that giveth unto the poor shall not lack: but he that hideth his eyes shall have many a curse.

Malachi 3:6-12

For I *am* the LORD, I change not; therefore ye sons of Jacob are not consumed. Even from the days of your fathers ye are gone away from mine ordinances, and have not kept *them.* Return unto me, and I will return unto you, saith the LORD of hosts. But ye said, Wherein shall we return? Will a man rob God? Yet ye have robbed me. But ye say, Wherein have we robbed thee? In tithes and offerings. Ye *are* cursed with a curse: for ye have robbed me, *even* this whole nation. Bring ye all the tithes into the storehouse, that there may be meat in mine house, and prove me now herewith, saith the LORD of hosts, if I will not open you the windows of heaven, and pour you out a blessing, that *there shall* not *be room* enough *to receive it.*And I will rebuke the devourer for your sakes, and he shall not destroy the fruits of your ground; neither shall your vine cast her fruit before the time in the field, saith the LORD of hosts. And all nations shall call you blessed: for ye shall be a delightsome land, saith the LORD of hosts.

Matthew 6:1-4

Take heed that ye do not your alms before men, to be seen of them: otherwise ye have no reward of your Father which is in heaven. Therefore when thou doest *thine* alms, do not sound a trumpet before thee, as the hypocrites do in the synagogues and in the streets, that they may have glory of men. Verily I say unto you, They have their reward. But when thou doest alms, let not thy left hand know what thy right hand doeth: That thine alms may be in secret: and thy Father which seeth in secret himself shall reward thee openly.

Matthew 23:23

Woe unto you, scribes and Pharisees, hypocrites! for ye pay tithe of mint and anise and cummin, and have omitted the weightier *matters* of the law, judgment, mercy, and faith: these ought ye to have done, and not to leave the other undone.

Luke 6:31-38

And as ye would that men should do to you, do ye also to them likewise. For if ye love them which love you, what thank have ye? for sinners also love those that love them. And if ye do good to them which do good to you, what thank have ye? For sinners also do even the same. And if ye lend *to them* of whom ye hope to receive, what thank have ye? for sinners also lend to sinners, to receive as much again. But love ye your enemies, and do good, and lend, hoping for nothing again; and your reward shall be great, and ye shall be the children of the Highest: for he is kind unto the unthankful and *to* the evil. Be ye therefore merciful, as your Father also is merciful. Judge not, and ye shall not be judged: condemn not, and ye shall not be condemned: forgive, and ye shall be forgiven: Give, and it shall be given unto you; good measure, pressed down, and shaken together, and running over, shall men give into your bosom. For with the same measure that ye mete withal it shall be measured to you again.

Acts 20:35

I have shewed you all things, how that so labouring ye ought to support the weak, and to remember the words of the Lord Jesus, how he said, It is more blessed to give than to receive.

2 Corinthians 9:6-7

But this *is true*, he that sows sparingly shall reap also sparingly; and he that sows in *the spirit of* blessing shall reap also in blessing: each according as he is purposed in his heart; not grievingly, or of necessity; for God loves a cheerful giver.

Galatians 6:9-10

But let us not lose heart in doing good; for in due time, if we do not faint, we shall reap. So then, as we have occasion, let us do good towards all, and specially towards those of the household of faith.

Ephesians 6:8

Knowing that whatsoever good thing any man doeth, the same shall he receive of the Lord, whether *he be* bond or free.

1 Timothy 6:17

Charge the rich in this world that they be not high-minded, nor trust in uncertain riches, but in the living God, He offering to us richly all things to enjoy, that they do good, that they be rich in good works, ready to share, to be generous, laying up in store for themselves a good foundation against the time to come, that they may lay hold on eternal life.

Hebrews 13:16

But do not forget to do good and to share, for with such sacrifices God is well pleased.

1 John 3:17-19

But whoever has this world's goods and sees his brother having need, and shuts up his bowels from him, how does the love of God dwell in him? My children, let us not love in word or in tongue, but in deed and in truth. And in this we shall know that we are of the truth, and shall assure our hearts before Him,

Faith and Obedience

Psalm 34:8-10

O taste and see that the LORD *is* good: blessed *is* the man *that* trusteth in him. O fear the LORD, ye his saints: for *there is* no want to them that fear him. The young lions do lack, and suffer hunger: but they that seek the LORD shall not want any good *thing.*

Proverbs 3:5-7

Trust in the LORD with all thine heart; and lean not unto thine own understanding. In all thy ways acknowledge him, and he shall direct thy paths. Be not wise in thine own eyes: fear the LORD, and depart from evil.

Numbers 23:19

God *is* not a man that He should lie, neither the son of man that He should repent. Has He said, and shall He not do it? Or has He spoken, and shall He not make it good?

2 Chronicles 20:20

And they rose early in the morning, and went forth into the wilderness of Tekoa: and as they went forth, Jehoshaphat stood and said, Hear me, O Judah, and ye inhabitants of Jerusalem; Believe in the LORD your God, so shall ye be established; believe his prophets, so shall ye prosper.

Isaiah 55:8-11

For my thoughts *are* not your thoughts, neither *are* your ways my ways, saith the LORD. For *as* the heavens are higher than the earth, so are my ways higher than your ways, and my thoughts than your thoughts. For as the rain cometh down, and the snow from heaven, and returneth not thither, but watereth the earth, and maketh it bring forth and bud, that it may give seed to the sower, and bread to the eater: So shall my word be that goeth forth out of my mouth: it shall not return unto me void, but it shall accomplish that which I please, and it shall prosper *in the thing* whereto I sent it.

Jeremiah 33:2-3

Thus saith the LORD the maker thereof, the LORD that formed it, to establish it; the LORD *is* his name; Call unto me, and I will answer thee, and shew thee great and mighty things, which thou knowest not.

Matthew 17:20

And Jesus said unto them, Because of your unbelief: for verily I say unto you, If ye have faith as a grain of mustard seed, ye shall say unto this mountain, Remove hence to yonder place; and it shall remove; and nothing shall be impossible unto you.

Matthew 19:26

But Jesus beheld *them,* and said unto them, With men this is impossible; but with God all things are possible.

Matthew 21:19-22

And when he saw a fig tree in the way, he came to it, and found nothing thereon, but leaves only, and said unto it, Let no fruit grow on thee henceforward for ever. And presently the fig tree withered away. And when the disciples saw *it,* they marvelled, saying, How soon is the fig tree withered away! Jesus answered and said unto them, Verily I say unto you, If ye have faith, and doubt not, ye shall not only do this *which is done* to the fig tree, but also if ye shall say unto this mountain, Be thou removed, and be thou cast into the sea; it shall be done. And all things, whatsoever ye shall ask in prayer, believing, ye shall receive.

Mark 9:23

Jesus said unto him, If thou canst believe, all things *are* possible to him that believeth.

Mark 11:23-24

For verily I say unto you, That whosoever shall say unto this mountain, Be thou removed, and be thou cast into the sea; and shall not doubt in his heart, but shall believe that those things which he saith shall come to pass; he shall have whatsoever he saith. Therefore I say unto you, What things soever ye desire, when ye pray, believe that ye receive *them,* and ye shall have *them.*

Romans 10:17

So then faith *cometh* by hearing, and hearing by the word of God.

Galatians 5:6

For in Jesus Christ neither circumcision availeth any thing, nor uncircumcision; but faith which worketh by love.

Hebrews 10:35-38

Cast not away therefore your confidence, which hath great recompense of reward. For ye have need of patience, that, after ye have done the will of God, ye might receive the promise. For yet a little while, and he that shall come will come, and will not tarry. Now the just shall live by faith: but if *any man* draw back, my soul shall have no pleasure in him.

Hebrews 11:1

Now faith is the assurance of things we hope for, the certainty of things we cannot see.

Hebrews 11:6

But without faith *it is* impossible to please *him:* for he that cometh to God must believe that he is, and *that* he is a rewarder of them that diligently seek him.

James 2:26

For as the body without the spirit is dead, so faith without works is dead also.

1 John 3:22

And whatsoever we ask, we receive of him, because we keep his commandments, and do those things that are pleasing in his sight.

1 John 5:14-15

And this is the confidence that we have in him, that, if we ask any thing according to his will, he heareth us: And if we know that he hear us, whatsoever we ask, we know that we have the petitions that we desired of him.

Unity and Agreement

Psalm 133:1-3

Behold, how good and how pleasant *it is* for brethren to dwell together in unity! *It is* like the precious ointment upon the head, that ran down upon the beard, *even* Aaron's beard: that went down to the skirts of his garments; As the dew of Hermon, *and as the dew* that descended upon the mountains of Zion: for there the LORD commanded the blessing, *even* life for evermore.

1 Corinthians 1:10

Now I beseech you, brethren, by the name of our Lord Jesus Christ, that ye all speak the same thing, and *that* there be no divisions among you; but *that* ye be perfectly joined together in the same mind and in the same judgment.

Philippians 2:2

Fulfill ye my joy, that ye be likeminded, having the same love, *being* of one accord, of one mind.

ENDNOTES

1   Viscott, David. M.D., Emotional Resilience: Simple Truths for Dealing with the Unfinished Business of Your Past

2   Businesstodayegypt.com

ABOUT THE AUTHOR

For over twelve years, Jason Hale—Entrepreneur, Business Owner, Financial Adviser, Founder of FaithPlanet.Net (An online prosperity resource) and Author of *Your Prosperity Blueprint*—has dedicated himself to helping people excel in every area of their lives. His ministry, speaking engagements, workshops and newly released book all work in consortium with this deeply rooted passion. Through the power of story-telling and the application of spiritual principles, Jason teaches corporate leaders, organizations, sales teams and individuals how to prosper in order to succeed.

Demonstrating the powerhouse that he is with innovative growth and sales strategies, Jason received sales training from Primerica Financial Services and within a record-breaking two years period advanced to Regional Vice President. He has since earned membership into the Financial Independence Council— an exclusive club of the highest income earners in Primerica.

More recently, Jason joined ING as a Career Representative. Within three years, while following the principles he writes about in his book, he supernaturally grew that business to 1,200 clients strong with tens of millions of dollars in assets under management.

Jason is married and has eight children. He has been a U.S. Army veteran since 1990 and an Ordained Minister since 1997. Jason spent almost six years as a Corrections Officer and Deputy Sheriff before launching his illustrious career in finances, where he has been recognized with over 100 sales awards.

BUY A SHARE OF THE FUTURE IN YOUR COMMUNITY

These certificates make great holiday, graduation and birthday gifts that can be personalized with the recipient's name. The cost of one S.H.A.R.E. or one square foot is $54.17. The personalized certificate is suitable for framing and will state the number of shares purchased and the amount of each share, as well as the recipient's name. The home that you participate in "building" will last for many years and will continue to grow in value.

Here is a sample SHARE certificate:

THIS CERTIFIES THAT

YOUR NAME HERE

HAS INVESTED IN A HOME FOR A DESERVING FAMILY

1985-2010

TWENTY-FIVE YEARS OF BUILDING FUTURES
IN OUR COMMUNITY ONE HOME AT A TIME

1200 SQUARE FOOT HOUSE @ $65,000 = $54.17 PER SQUARE FOOT
This certificate represents a tax deductible donation. It has no cash value.

YES, I WOULD LIKE TO HELP!

*I support the work that Habitat for Humanity does and I want to be part of the excitement! As a donor, I will receive periodic updates on your construction activities but, more importantly, I know my gift will help a family in our community realize the dream of homeownership. **I would like to SHARE in your efforts against substandard housing in my community!** (Please print below)*

PLEASE SEND ME _____ SHARES at $54.17 EACH = $ $_____

In Honor Of: _____

Occasion: (Circle One)   HOLIDAY   BIRTHDAY   ANNIVERSARY

     OTHER: _____

Address of Recipient: _____

Gift From: _____ *Donor Address:* _____

Donor Email: _____

I AM ENCLOSING A CHECK FOR $ $_____ PAYABLE TO HABITAT FOR HUMANITY OR PLEASE CHARGE MY VISA OR MASTERCARD (CIRCLE ONE)

Card Number _____ Expiration Date: _____

Name as it appears on Credit Card _____ Charge Amount $ _____

Signature _____

Billing Address _____

Telephone # Day _____ Eve _____

PLEASE NOTE: Your contribution is tax-deductible to the fullest extent allowed by law.
Habitat for Humanity • P.O. Box 1443 • Newport News, VA 23601 • 757-596-5553
www.HelpHabitatforHumanity.org